M000315440

"**Phil and Cindy Smith dared to ask**: Can I risk being misunderstood, being different, or being with hurting people for the sake of the gospel? How much do I really love people? Not just the cleaned up church crowd, but the needy, hurting and dirty people of the world?

Their answer, beautifully told in *Would You Like To Put Your Shoes In My Closet*, takes us on a journey that is not just inspiring but transforming. Phil and Cindy's roots are surprisingly entwined with many other influential, well-known leaders. Their history is important for us to retrace because it helps us understand God's ongoing work in the world today. This amazing true story defines what it means to love and follow Jesus and others. Read it and join the adventure!"

Mark and Jan Foreman
Pastor and wife of NORTH COAST CALVARY CHURCH
Carlsbad, CA
Author of WHOLLY JESUS and NEVER SAY NO: RAISING BIG-PICTURE KIDS

"**Corrie Ten Boom's advice to Cindy and Phil Smith**, to choose a country which was under persecution, and begin to pray for the people, led quite naturally to having a "ministry of presence" with the followers of Brother Andrew and others.

This book has a sweetness, simplicity and gentleness that makes me hungry to recapture the newness of discovering Jesus, as I first did when I met Him years ago in my early 20's in Cambridge, England.

Now, I am 80 years of age and thinking about the delight I found bringing a smile to His face and knowing His kiss on my cheek, as I simply learned to "trust and obey".

Thank you Cindy for reminding me that 'you can't measure ministry with metrics'. How indeed do you count success? Only by the still small voice…unmistakable but insistent in the deep place where nobody goes.

Try it - it is true.

This is not only a good read, it is a MUST read. You won't be sorry.

Jill Briscoe
Teacher and author

"**Cindy and Phil Smith** have lived a life together that not many have experienced. As a young seminary student in Chicago, Phil was seeking God's will for his life. *Should he become a military chaplain, a pastor or a missionary?* When he was smitten by a feisty young girl, Cindy, who was training to be a teacher to missionary children. His proposal to her "would you like to put your shoes in my closet?" was the beginning of a lifelong love affair and adventure together.

Through the many years of difficulties in raising a family while in ministry, and then carrying the gospel to 'closed areas' of the world, they remained in love with Jesus, His work and each other!

This is an inspiring story for all."

Karen and Tass Saada
Author of ONCE AN ARAFAT MAN and founder and directors of Hope for Ishmael
Newark, MO

"**The story is a beautiful challenge on how to finish well.** This book is not just a story about ministry and believers living under persecution, it is the story of two lives well lived - a story that will challenge the reader to do likewise."

Dr. Jody Dillow
BEE WORLD President Emeritus

"**Phil Smith was my pastor** when I came to faith in Jesus in San Clemente, CA back in 1976. I was discipled by Cindy and I went on to study in Multnomah Bible College where I met my husband.

The one statement that has most inspired and challenged me is: "What if the church in America was required to share last week's sermon or Bible study with five others before being allowed to be taught more from the Word?"

Phil and Cindy taught this rule to those they trained in the underground church. They must be taught to share with others. Inspiring!"

Jill Ann Habig Mitchell

"**I read the entire manuscript in a week**. I could NOT put it down! It is amazing to see what God has done in the lives of this dedicated couple."

Betsy Ahlberg
Travel consultant, Alamo World Travel

"**A beautiful life story.** We can be encouraged by it today."

Hank Paulson
Director of 4-D MINISTRIES (formerly called EEBM working out of Holland)

"**I met Chaplain Smith in England** on my first active duty assignment.

I was invited to teach a Bible study class as part of his ministry. Soon Phil and Cindy became our close friends.

We are always amazed at what they dared for Christ's sake, and how they touched lives for Him in places where angels fear to walk. Their enduring love for each other and for Christ is an inspiring and heartwarming story."

Herb White, Lt.Col, USAF Ret.

Would You Like to Put Your Shoes in My Closet?

By Cindy Smith

Cover Design: Matthew Lawler

Layout: Ray Fowler

Editor: Ginny Stephen

ISBN: 978-0-9883813-2-2

Matthew Lawler Creative *Publishing*

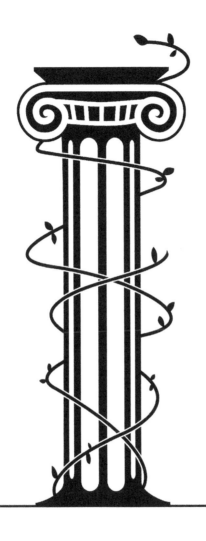

The Pillar and the Vines that Phil drew for Cindy.

Table of Contents

Introduction

For over two thousand years millions of Christ-followers have heeded His exhortation to make disciples, and by doing this, they have helped elevate the life of man on earth. Most are unknown to history; have never written a book or had a book written about them. Nevertheless their faithful lives have modeled Christ's way of life for multitudes, and they will find themselves highly honored by their King at the Final Gathering. Phil and Cindy Smith are two of those millions, and I am honored to say a few words of introduction about their story.

We first met the Smith's when they came to join the staff of BEE (Biblical Education by Extension) in Vienna, Austria. We were involved in leading a covert, extension biblical training program behind the Iron Curtain from 1978 to 1994. Phil and Cindy entered our lives at a critical time. We were struggling with the "teenage challenge" with two of our teenagers, and were much in need of help. . Linda and I were the oldest people on our team. At last we had an "older couple" who could give us counsel and perspective. Those hours spent with them were incredibly important in our lives and bonded us together in ministry for the next 25 years.

As I turned the last page of Cindy's account of her life with Phil this morning, tears came to my eyes as my mind returned to those years when we worked together in Romania, Russia, Poland, Vietnam and other communist countries. Cindy's keen eye for cultural detail and lively writing style vividly brought to life the wonderful stories of the hundreds she and Phil ministered to during the communist era. These stories will challenge you, as they did me, to think about the final meaning of our lives. The sacrifices made by the believers in Eastern Europe and Russia; the persecutions they endured, and the utter economic and cultural catastrophe foisted upon them by ruthless dictatorships created in them a vigorous and inspiring faith. Phil and Cindy would agree that during the communist era, they met some of the most wonderful people in the history of God's army.

The story began on a beach in the Philippines during WW2 where Phil served in the Navy. On that beach, Phil trusted Christ. He then decided to go to Seminary, where he met Cindy and asked her to marry him with an unusual proposal, "Why don't you just put your shoes in my closet and help me figure out what I am to do?" Eventually, Cindy agreed and this began a whirlwind life of amazing faithfulness and ministry impact, a life story you will be blessed to read.

Phil served as a military Chaplain and as a pastor of churches in California and Colorado. Then, in the early 1980's began his ministry behind the Iron Curtain. Scores of ministry trips to Romania, Poland, Hungary, Russia and other countries followed. During that time they introduced hundreds of thirsty believers to biblical courses on marriage, Romans and Galatians, the Christian Life, How to Study the Bible and many others. Equally important was their personal ministry in which they solidified marriages, gave wise counsel, led many to Christ, and conducted marriage ceremonies. You will be amazed at the stories of encounters with the security police and escapes from danger. You will see God's hand of provision and protection, and your life will be enriched as your read about His answers to prayer and care for His people.

Cindy was instrumental in helping to begin something new in those countries - women's ministry. She trained women how to teach the scriptures to other women and to their children.

As you read these pages, you will be a witness to history through the eyes of a couple who experienced it. The failure of the communist system eventually led to its overthrow. You will witness the transition to freedom and see the long lasting effect of the Smith's work after the wall fell. Thousands of new churches were formed. BEE trained over 25,000 students in the underground church. In Romania alone, over 1,200 BEE students emerged after the system collapsed, and took over hundreds of churches.

After four trips to Russia and functioning as the first pastor of a new church in Moscow, at 70 years of age, the Smith's began a new mission – to Vietnam, Burma, and Ukraine. As a child, Phil would pray for Burma and in the final season of his life was able to serve in ministry there.

Cindy relates many stories about believers living in Vietnam: their joy, their response to persecution, and example will challenge you to ask, "What am I living for?"

In his late 70's Phil asked Cindy to write out a list of what she would like to do over the next fifteen years if the Lord continued to give them good health. One of those items was a return to the beach where he first came to know Christ. While attending a BEE conference the Philippines, he was able to do that.

Among the items on their "bucket list" were a return to the countries where they had ministered to encourage the believers they had met. They also wanted to maximize their marriage. For many years they kept a little fish bowl in the kitchen filled with ideas they had written down for a day out together, and they would take turns selecting from the bowl.

As the twilight came, Phil was diagnosed with Alzheimer's. The story of their final years is a beautiful challenge on how to finish well. This book is not just a story about ministry and believers living under persecution, it is the story of two lives well-lived; a story that will challenge the reader to do likewise. The last words of great men are often significant. The last words of the Apostle Paul give us a fitting summary of Phil and Cindy's lives.

> *I have fought the good fight, I have finished the race, I have kept the faith. Now there is in store for me the crown of righteousness, which the Lord, the righteous Judge, will award to me on that day—and not only to me, but also to all who have longed for his appearing. 2 Timothy 4:7-8*

I commend this book to you. You will be a better person for reading it.

Dr. Joseph (Jody) Dillow

BEE WORLD President Emeritus

Our Testimonies

Phil Smith's Testimony and Early Life

I was born on September 30, 1926 in Grand Ledge, Michigan. My father was the pastor of the First Baptist Church of Grand Ledge and I was born in the parsonage, right next door to the church. As I started going to church at about two weeks of age, I have literally been attending church all my life.

When I was seven years old, my father was the pastor of the Congregational church in Whitehall, Michigan. Every summer he would invite guest evangelists to come and hold meetings for several weeks. I don't remember the name of the evangelist or what he preached about in the summer of 1933, but I remember being convinced that I was a sinner and needed to accept Jesus into my heart to be "saved."

When the evangelist gave the invitation, I was the first one down the aisle to declare my decision for Christ. My parents were moved to tears and I had no doubt that Jesus came into my heart and that I was truly 'born again'.

My father's tradition was to baptize new converts in the Duck Lake channel that emptied into Lake Michigan. Believers from the church stood on the shore and sang hymns while 10 or 12 of us were baptized that day.

As a child, I was aware of what sin was, but I struggled at times to do what was right. My parents held an annual Sunday school picnic complete with games, foot races, bag races and so on. During the depression, in 1935 when I was 9 years old, my parents had somehow managed to buy all kinds of candy to be used as prizes for the game winners.

In the backseat of my dad's Model T Ford, were all these goodies! A buddy and I thought we would just snitch a little bit, so we started eating the Hershey bars, which were to be the grand prize for the ultimate winners. Of course we could not stop until we ate them all! My parents were so upset that someone had stolen the candy bars that I was too embarrassed to tell them that my buddy and I were the culprits. I never did tell them!

On another occasion, when I was 11 or 12 we had a cat that had recently had kittens. While my parents were busy with guests, I decided the kittens needed to be baptized. As the child of a Baptist minister, I knew all about baptism! So, one by one I baptized them in a barrel filled with rainwater - in the name of the Father, The Son and the Holy Spirit. After submerging each one, I handed them to my buddy to dry with a towel.

When finished, I went upstairs and told my parents, thinking they would be proud of me! I was sure mistaken about that! I had a feeling that when mom and dad went to bed that evening, they had a good laugh about my kitty baptisms.

But my worst childhood prank of all happened at a wedding. A couple having their wedding at our church parked their car in front of the church, unattended. I don't know where I got the idea, but my buddy and I let the air out of all four of the tires! Boy, were they ever mad when they came out of the church!

 I am so grateful that the Lord has mercy and forgives us for our crimes! Due to the privilege of having Christian parents who loved me and encouraged me to read and study God's Word, I was able to grow in my faith. My first Bible was given to me by my parents when I was ten years old and both my brother and I were in a boys Sunday school class taught by my father for many years.

The annual Vacation Bible School that my parents held was one of my greatest times of spiritual development. Learning memory verses laid a solid foundation for me in the scriptures. Those truths anchored me through grade school, high school, and beyond.

I attended two years of high school in Michigan when my parents decided they wanted me to get a Christian education and helped me and my brother get scholarships to Bob Jones Academy. We worked in the kitchen, doing dishes and waiting on tables in the student dining room. I thoroughly enjoyed that year: the Lord was working in my heart and teaching me to be thankful.

When I finished High School in 1944, World War II was in full swing. I knew that if I didn't volunteer, I would be drafted. So, with my parent's reluctant permission, I enlisted in the U.S. Navy, and was sent to boot camp at the Great Lakes Naval Training Center in Illinois and then Basic Engineering School and finally the

Navy Diesel Training School in Richmond, VA.

I left for the Navy in September of 1944 and was assigned to my barracks at the naval training Center. Each room held about 100 bunks, so I had 99 roommates! There were no closets: everything we owned was kept in our Navy Sea bags, tied to a pipe near our bunk.

There were no washing machines or dryers, so we washed our clothes by hand in the washroom. The military discipline of keeping the ship spotlessly clean was part of Navy life. Our NCO would turn on the lights in the middle of the night yelling… "Hit the deck – get a piece of steel wool under your foot and steel wool the deck!" We would jump out of bed and clean until a trainer came to inspect our work.

As a Christian, I was always hoping to meet other born-again believers. In the Mess Hall I would bow my head to give thanks for the food and other believers would see me, or I would notice them praying. This led to us becoming friends and encouraging one another.

Training at the Diesel Engine school was intense, equipping us to handle mechanic duties aboard invasion boats. The final exam required each group of three recruits to take a diesel engine apart piece by piece and then be timed to see how fast we could put it all back together! Our reward was a weekend of liberty…if the engine would work.

Fortunately, my team succeeded and I was promoted to Seaman First Class and received orders to a Navy Sea Bee outfit bound for the Philippines. We packed our Sea bags and were taken by train to a Navy transport ship in San Francisco.

The former cargo ship was terribly crowded with over 5000 people on board. With no dining tables or chairs, we stood to eat with our trays loaded with food. It was not a pleasant trip: the ship was always rolling in heavy seas. Some men sat quietly and read, while other gathered in small groups to play cards. With my training I was called to serve below deck in the engine room and was ordered to keep all the brass pipes and fixtures polished!

Working in the 'bowels' of the ship was scary for me. Travelling through waters patrolled by Japanese submarines, I would look at the iron sides of the ship and realize that I could be polishing brass below sea level when we could be hit with a Japanese torpedo! My prayer life got stronger!!

Our ship was escorted by three heavily armed destroyer class ships. One day, a general alarm was sounded. Our ship's radar had detected a group of explosive mines floating directly ahead, so the destroyers sped up and exploded the mines. While it was exciting to see the explosions, I was grateful for the Lord's protection.

Twenty-eight days later, we arrived in the Philippines. Bunking at a tent city I learned right away to never leave my boots under my cot. The tropical rainstorms that swept through overnight would wash my boots far away!

Assigned to a SEA BEE outfit at the end of Calicoan Island, I shared my new home, a Quonset hut, with 15 other men. The floors were raised and the sides were screened and at each corner of the tent was a 50 gallon oil drum that captured rainwater. This was where we did our personal washing and laundry.

After several months working on the pontoon assembly line, I was assigned to operate a 10-ton crane with a 40-foot boom in order to unload heavy boxes of beams and bolts for the pontoon assembly process. I was only 19 years old and I had a crew of 15 young sailors helping me!

One special friend during my time at the camp was Chaplain Bill Simons – after the war he returned to the Philippines as a missionary. Our camp had a well-equipped hobby and woodworking shop and I made a pair of candleholders out of caliber shells. I also had a pet spider monkey named Mabel who kept me company and entertained my friends. Often she would get into trouble stealing cigarette lighters!

When the Japanese surrendered to the USA in 1945 the sailors who had been in the Navy the longest were the first to return home. Our work in those last days was to destroy equipment, until the U.S. government decided to give some to the Philippine government.

Finally, I received my orders to return home and in mid May of 1946 our ship sailed under the San Francisco Bay Bridge. It was a cold and cloudy day, but our ship was full of very happy sailors!

I had phoned my parents and purposely lied about when I would be coming home - I wanted to surprise them by arriving a day earlier than they expected me. I will never do that again! In the military, we were served so much Spam (a meat product in a can) that we were sick of it. I had asked my mother to never serve it to me again. However, because I came home early she was so surprised that she served Spam on my first night home from the war!

I praise the Lord for His protection and care for me during those 30 months of active duty. The spiritual training I had received and the truths I had learned from my Bible reading were what kept me close to the Lord through all of my Navy experiences. It was while I was serving in the South Pacific that I began to feel that God was calling me to full time Christian service.

One very pleasant, sunny day, yielding to the constraining leadership of the Holy Spirit, I knelt on the beach and committed my life wholly to Jesus Christ. I said, "Lord, if you will bring me safely home from this war, I will serve you all the rest of the days of my life." The Lord graciously answered that prayer!

Cindy's Testimony and Early Life

I was born on July 1, 1932 in an Iowa farmhouse to Sandy and Miriam Cleveland and big brother Paul. After my Aunt Letha led my father to Jesus, he was determined to become a preacher, so my family moved to Chicago. Northern Baptist Seminary was to be our new home!

One of my earliest memories was the drive to Chicago with David, my baby brother's high chair tied on top of the car. My parents had very little money, but lots of faith - a family friend drove us all the way to Chicago as we had no car.

The elevated train was just outside the windows of our tiny 3 room apartment in Taft Hall and my parents made a bed for me on the floor of the kitchen. The rules were that if you had more than three children you had to find housing elsewhere: so we only qualified for a little while…

Soon Lois was born, and then Martha Jane, and then baby sister Judy! All the while Dad was finishing both college and seminary training. Sometimes he worked 3 or more jobs while Mother taught piano lessons and raised vegetables on a rented garden plot. One of Dad's jobs was operating an elevator in an apartment building and we were so proud of his nice uniform!

When Mom was busy with the babies I would go to church with Dad and sit in the balcony of Tabernacle Baptist Church. I was allowed to copy down words, but no picture drawing! On the front of the pulpit was a scarf with words on it that I was allowed to copy: *Ye Must be Born Again.*

Since there was a new baby at home and I thought our doctor had brought her to our house, I asked Daddy to explain about how a person could be born again: does the doctor do it? He explained it this way……

> *"You are a gift from God to Mommy and me. Your name is Elizabeth Cleveland and you will always be a Cleveland - nothing can ever change that. So wherever you go, whatever you do, stand up tall and make me proud because being a Cleveland and my daughter is very special.*

> *However, somewhere out there is a young man whom you will marry. Your mother and I are praying for him now, even though we don't know his name. When you marry him, you*

*will take his name. Whatever you do, wherever you go, you will
want to make him proud you are his wife – and you will have
two names!*

*But there is another name that is even more important and
special; that is the name of Christian. One day Jesus will knock
on your heart's door and you will invite him to come in and
be your personal Lord and Savior and then your name will be
Christian -.a Christ follower! You will know when that day
comes and that is called being born again!"*

When I was almost ten years old, our family moved to South
Dakota to be 'home missionaries' to a number of little beginning
churches on the prairie. Dad was pastor for eight churches at one
time! We would be on the North part of the ministry for two
weeks and then the South for two weeks.

The churches met in homes, old dance halls and little church
buildings. The initial work was begun by the American Sunday
School Union and now the fledgling churches needed leadership
development and training.

I helped Daddy with the little children, teaching Bible stories, but
remember feeling that I was pretending to be someone that I was
not. I did not yet have Jesus in my heart and I felt guilty. I could
tell other children about Jesus but had not yet invited him into my
heart.

One day my dad asked me if I was ready to accept Jesus. I was
shocked that he knew! Going off to a quiet place, I invited Jesus
into my heart and life and went to tell Daddy. I was so surprised
when he called my mom and said that we would have a party

because this was my second birthday! Daddy had a big baptism planned for the 4th of July at a nearby dam, so he baptized my brothers and me there!

What an adventure we were living, having moved from downtown Chicago, to the tiny prairie town of Union Center and a house with no running water or electricity. We went to school in a one-room schoolhouse where the older kids helped the younger ones, while the teacher taught new material. You learned to concentrate on your own work, no matter what else was going on in the room!

Some of the prairie kids worked as sheep herders. What a wonderful life I thought that was - to be able to ride your horse over the gentle hills and move the sheep from place to place. I was allowed to go herding with some friends and spent time laying in the sun and talking. But I was a bit of a snob- I liked to impress my friends by telling them about life in Chicago! I would show them our pop up toaster, and electric mixer to impress them…

I wanted to spend a night with one girl who lived in a sod house and never understood why my parents did not want me to go. When they finally relented, I had a great time until I awakened, feeling something biting me.

My mother inspected me carefully when I came home, and sure enough, I had fleabites and lice. I remember that I was not to tell my friend what happened, and I also remember my mother burning some of my clothes!

Just a few yards from our house was a small stream under the cottonwood trees. Even though the streambed was often dry, it was still a delightful place for us to play. If you were to ask me what is the most pleasant memory place I could think of - it would be the soft breezes underneath those cottonwood trees in that little gully in Union Center where we played!

Living on the prairie was hard work: one distinct memory is of watching my father and his friends butcher a calf, and also witnessing the pheasant and deer hunting which kept our family alive. We tried some gardening but it was not easy to keep the rabbits and other varmints away.

My brothers, David and Paul worked hard in a small dairy business in Owanka, South Dakota, on the south end of the parish. I do not know how they managed to milk the cows, separate the milk, sterilize bottles and deliver the fresh milk to the half dozen homes in our little town…but they did.

My mother sewed all of our clothes: I recall one Christmas when all 8 of us had nice warm flannel pajamas that she had made. I wonder now how she kept that project a secret - I never saw even one scrap of flannel before Christmas.

Dad heard about a camp in the Black Hills, which was struggling for leadership during those war years. Camp Judson was our summer home for the next 12 years. Mother became the camp cook, nurse, counselor and mother to all!

My jobs were; peeling potatoes, cleaning out cabins, and checking groups in. I remember that I was always looking for the good-looking boys and I had new pen pals after many camps. They did not last though and I soon forgot what they looked like.

I was deeply touched by the missionaries who came to be with us during those summers. During this time I told the Lord that If He wanted to use me, I would become a missionary. I did *not* want to become a pastor's wife— I believed that anyone could do that and that the Lord *needed* missionaries.

I am sure that those early years of watching my parents pray with folks who came to talk with them about so many needs touched my heart. I can still see them kneeling beside the couch to lead a couple to Jesus. I knew that serving God was the greatest thing anyone could do.

We seldom saw our families back East any longer, and grew to love the folks out on the prairie as they became our new family. I praise the Lord for those early years of learning to trust God and to make moves and adjustments - they were lessons that have served me well.

Hardships were part of our lives as well: my older brother was often sick and my sister Lois died when I was a teen, which affected my mother deeply. She had to care for six kids with various illnesses in an area without doctors nearby.

I was the only one in the family that did not get rheumatic fever. When I was in High school, there was a terrible epidemic of polio and most of the school's activities were closed down. I got a job filling supper trays in the local hospital's kitchen, so that I could be close to my sister who was in a room upstairs. She died there with Daddy and me with her.

During those difficult years, some college credits were offered in a nearby college. As there was a shortage of schoolteachers on the prairie, I chose that training. In my day, you could marry a rancher, take nursing training in Minneapolis, or choose teaching!

My parents moved to Arizona hoping the climate would improve the health of my brothers and sisters. I had to finish school on my own but I saw it as just another adventure.

My folks bought me two white suitcases with red trim and I moved into the home of a retired missionary and his wife. They were childless, so I am sure I was a challenge to them.

I went to summer school in Sioux Falls College and then back to the prairie to teach school, while taking courses at Black Hills Teacher College. I had many friends and enjoyed singing for church meetings and school functions and even wrote and directed a Christmas play.

To finish my preparation for teaching missionary kids, I needed to go to Chicago to Northwest Seminary. My studies were Cross Culture Studies. I was warmly welcomed there by the President, as a 'second generation student'. Perhaps, Sandy Cleveland with his six kids and his 10 years of study was a bit difficult to forget!

Hello Chicago, again! Little did I know who I would meet....

CHAPTER ONE

Coming Together As One

Genesis 2:24: "For this reason a man will leave his father and mother and be united to his wife, and they will become one flesh."

After completing my school teaching year in South Dakota, I traveled to Arizona to visit my parents. My father was leading Christian camps in the mountains and I helped for a while and then traveled on to Chicago, planning to teach missionary kids.

Arriving at Northern Baptist Seminary, I was met by the school President and stayed in their guest room for a few weeks. As I had lived on campus until I was 10, many of the professors were friends of my family.

My father had often invited students from 'Northern' to spend time in South Dakota with us, working in various ministries. Several of these young men were still attending the seminary and were preparing to join a summer mission trip to Japan. Phil Smith was a part of this team. The team drove across the USA to California, speaking in churches along the way, and raising funds for their trip.

When the group returned to Chicago I met them and heard their reports. Although I must have met Phil then, I honestly do not remember that meeting. But Phil told me that he never forgot our first meeting!

Phil was speaking at churches on the weekends about his summer ministry in Japan and some of us were recruited to join a gospel team to go with Phil- I was part of a singing trio. When we met to pray before our ministries, we were asked to share what was on our hearts that day....

I shared that I needed wisdom to select the right roommate in the women's dorm. Many of the women were older, returning mission-aries and very settled in their ways. I was a bit fearful of them - I was the new young kid!

Many of the women were named Elizabeth, and it seemed that all the nicknames were already chosen; Betty, Betsy, Beth, and Liz were gone. I ended up being called 'Blackie' because my hair was black, but I was hurt because we had a cow named 'Blackie'! So they settled on calling me Cinders and it was Phil who shortened it to Cindy!

Phil's prayer request was for wisdom in deciding between training for the mission field, the pastorate or the military chaplaincy! After hearing my simple request for a roommate, he leaned over and whispered, "Why don't you just put your shoes in my closet and help me figure out what I am to do?"

I was shocked by his words and began to distance myself from this guy. After all, what did I know about him? He had been in the war and in the Philippines and he came from Michigan.....each of these factors were very distant to my understanding.

But every day as I went to the dining room for lunch it seemed that the only chair not occupied was next to Phil Smith. I didn't catch on for a long time that the interruptions that delayed me as we waited for the dining room doors to open were planned by Phil's friends!

One weekend, our gospel team was invited to Phil's home church in Muskegon, Michigan. Pastor Wilbur Welch warmly welcomed Phil. I could tell that he was proud of Phil and I also became aware that several most attractive women were also interested in welcoming Phil!

Phil's parents were warm and loving and their home reminded me of my own. Both were active in Child Evangelism Fellowship: Phil's mother was an artist whose work illustrated many materials used to teach children. Some of those materials had found their way to my parents' ministry in South Dakota! Michigan and South Dakota didn't seem so far away from each other!

After that visit, Phil took on a whole new look to me. We began meeting almost nightly in a classroom for prayer and walked many Sunday afternoons in a park near the Seminary. We discussed what life would be like in each one of the ministries Phil was considering.

He often repeated his request that I put my shoes in his closet.... I told him once that I would only embarrass him if I were to become a military chaplain's wife as I would not know who to salute! Phil told me that was HIS job, not mine, and also told me that he would give me my own missionary kids to teach!

Having grown up as a preacher's kid, I wanted to experience life on my own, and travel and serve the Lord. I was not afraid of hardship or adventure - I just did not want to be *just* a preacher's wife. I felt anyone could do that!

My struggle was with my own will, because it was obvious that God had placed Phil in my life for a reason. There wasn't anything about Phil that I did not admire: he was deeply committed to Christ, full of adventure, generous, caring and loving with his parents. I knew I needed to obey God's plan for my life and it became clear that Phil was part of that plan.

One of our favorite Seminary professors was a long time friend of my father, (who asked him for some background information about Phil.) I guess the response was favorable because Dr. and Mrs. Filkin hosted an engagement party for us.

Sending out a letter to our friends, Dr. Filkin told them only that there was to be a very serious discussion to be held in his apartment and the contents of this letter were not to be discussed with anyone!

He began the "meeting" with a lengthy presentation about the affairs of the world and how important it was to consider the important events of our day. Phil and I had been told to arrive late and ring the doorbell at a certain time.

As we entered Dr. Filkin stopped, saying that the real reason for the meeting was to announce that Phil had proposed to me and we were there to celebrate. Our friends were excited and shocked as no one had any idea that we were going to be engaged.

The romantic part of the evening came underneath the noisy elevated train when Phil gave me my diamond, telling me that he could give it to me again in the park if I wished! That's my Phil!

Our wedding was held in May at Phil's home church in Muskegon with my family travelling from Arizona and our seminary friends as our attendants. After one night of a honeymoon we got word that Phil's beloved aunt had died and we left for the funeral.

CHAPTER TWO

Beginning as One

Philippians 1:4-5: "In all my prayers for all of you, I always pray with joy, because of your partnership in the gospel from the first day until now, being confident of this; the he who began a good work in you will carry it on to completion until the day of Christ Jesus."

Our first home was a one-room basement apartment in a building across the street from the Seminary. We had a 'Murphy bed', and a tiny closet kitchen. A bathroom and a walk in closet (which became our daughter Becky's first bedroom) completed our space.

While Phil was finishing seminary, we were both working at Hartford Fire Insurance and were surprised when the company president called us in for an appointment. The President was a believer and wanted to know our future plans. After hearing that Phil had applied for chaplain positions as well as looking into churches in Michigan, the President surprised us again by asking us how much we owed for our school bills and other expenses.

Phil gave him a rough number and he wrote us a check to cover our expenses, saying that he wanted us to be free to serve wherever the Lord led us!

We were shocked to learn that shortly after that meeting he died of a heart attack. When we went back to his office to ask his secretary how we should repay the money, she told us that he often did this for seminary students and that we should remember his encouragement and 'pay it forward'!

Serving our First Church

Our first church was in Grand Blanc, Michigan. We moved into the partially furnished parsonage with all we owned packed in a station wagon! Looking out the window of our kitchen we could see Army tanks in the field behind our house, since the auto industry was building military vehicles.

Our son Timothy was born during our time in Grand Blanc and he and his sister Becky had many wonderful baby sitters from the church.

While in Grand Blanc, Phil received his call for the chaplaincy. He was excited to travel to San Antonio for training, driving me to South Dakota to spend the winter with my parents. It was great for the grandparents to have time with us before we shipped off to England.

Off to England

On arrival at Sculthorpe Air Force Base we did not immediately have military housing available so we lived in a hotel for a few months with other military families - I remember cooking our meals on the floor using an electric fry pan!

Later we were housed in an old mansion, Guist Hall, about 60 miles from the base. Two other families shared this old mansion, which was owned by the Sir Thomas Cook family (of the Cooks Travel tours). The other family had children and we all had a great time playing together. Becky and Tim began school and developed an English accent! Our son Daniel was born at the base hospital on Easter morning and life was good!

Phil began an evangelistic team of military men who conducted services in nearby towns. We also enjoyed a small group Bible study in our own home. Folks came to Christ, ministered to each other and some even continued in service for the Lord after their military service.

Phil was feeling challenged by the military, but loved it. Unfortunately, his was an *uncertain* contract with the military. He had signed papers for *definite* status, but somehow the papers were lost. As there seemed to be an overage of Baptists in the military chaplaincy Phil was sent back to the USA.

We prayed with our group about what to do and where to live. My parents were hoping for South Dakota, and Phil's parents wanted us to settle in Michigan, but I remembered flying into Colorado Springs - and thinking, *this is the most beautiful place.* The Air Force was beginning a new Academy there and it would be a good place for Phil to continue in the Air Force reserves. So we asked the Lord for a church to serve in Colorado Springs.

Colorado Springs

The folks in our small group were amazed when we received a letter from a struggling church in Colorado Springs, asking us to come for a visit. We had the military send our belongings to Colorado, flew to visit our families, left our children with my parents and went to Colorado.

We loved the new church building, but learned that as the church owed a lot of money to local businesses they could hardly pay us a salary, but they could let us use their tiny parsonage! In those early days the folks of the church were so committed, they even took out personal loans to pay the construction bills.

We moved into the tiny house and Phil worked at a small Convenience store/filling station for a bit, while church members picked up our bill for milk and eggs, giving sacrificially to make it all work. We enjoyed our days at Temple Baptist Church, leading some fun Christmas programs, and creative vacation Bible school programs. Both Phil and I wrote much of the curriculum and small group materials in those days.

During our tenure in Colorado Springs, our son, Joel David arrived. Our friend and neighbor, Dr. Diffee, delivered him at the local hospital. Moving out of the small parsonage, we bought our first house and were later able to host Brother Andrew and his friend Corrie ten Boom. This was when we first began praying for the persecuted church behind the Iron Curtain!

Meeting Corrie

The local churches had formed a fellowship to sponsor city-wide weeks of special meetings. One of the speakers turned out to be Brother Andrew, who became a frequent and much loved guest in our home and he introduced us to Corrie ten Boom, also from Holland.

Corrie would ask to pray with me and sought to encourage me as a young wife and mother. One day she spread out a map of the world and asked me to choose a country behind the Iron Curtain and begin praying for the persecuted believers in that country as well as the country's leaders. I chose Bulgaria because it seemed easier to spell than Czechoslovakia!

She told me to ask the Lord to show me what he wanted me to know about the country and the people: it was an interesting challenge! I began praying for Bulgaria and one day Phil brought home a pastor from Bulgaria who had stopped by the church. We became friends and before he returned home, he gave me candelabra, which he had made. It serves as a reminder to me that nothing is done without prayer first!

Phil took Corrie to a new coffee house ministry on the nearby military base. Guests were invited to sing, read poetry or tell jokes. Phil waited with Corrie while others had their turn and told me later that when she went up front, he heard a little chuckle in the crowd as this funny little old lady from Holland moved to the microphone. The audience grew silent when she began with, "I am here tonight to tell you about my time in prison!"

She told the audience how she and her family had been imprisoned by the Nazis for harboring Jews during World War II; and went on to speak about her time in the Ravensbruck concentration camp and the ways that God used her and her sister during the most difficult days of her life.

While she had prayed for protection from imprisonment, God had answered her prayers with a "No," in order that she and her sister could share Jesus Christ with many prisoners who had never heard of him. She finished by inviting the audience to accept Christ as their Savior and allow Him to lead in their lives. Many responded!

Seeds are Planted

Phil told me that when he was in the Philippines with the Navy he was lonely and asked God to give him a friend. He would pull out his New Testament and begin to read, noticing how some people would pull away from him while others would come to him with their problems and fears.

He saw how powerful the pages of God's Word were: the Word ministers to us and calls people to Himself. He said, "I am never alone with His Word in my heart, on my mind and lips."

Phil once found a Bible that a church leader had left behind in the church. Calling him midweek, Phil asked how his week was going. The man seemed confused until Phil told him that he was worried that the man had not even missed his Bible!

It was these experiences that the Lord used to urge us to pray for those without a copy of the Bible, and for those Brother Andrew had told us about who were printing pages of the Bible on their own secret printing presses.

It was difficult for us to understand how those in leadership in closed countries had such a hatred for the Bible. I recall the testimony of Luci in Russia who told me that she could not understand why her country's leaders were so angry over pages written so long ago. She said it made her all the more curious to read the Bible for herself.

After Colorado Springs we had a short stay at a church in Aurora, and then on to a church in Chandler, Arizona. Both of these churches had strong and committed workers and were seeking to serve the Lord more than tradition!

On to California

While on vacation in California Phil was asked to speak at a church in San Clemente; with the proposal offered: If he would speak for two Sundays at a church without a pastor, they would give us a free place to stay at the beach!

What family could overlook that?

In church, a gentleman seated behind us asked the kids if we were going to Disneyland. They told him yes - the very next morning. He told us to meet him at the gate and he would have something special for us! It turned out that Mr. Scott worked at Global Van Line, adjacent to Disneyland and he gave us a pass for an entire week in Disneyland!

Later the same church asked Phil to come speak for a week and the kids asked him to see if a house in Dana Point (which we had visited) was still an Open House/ Model home. The kids were praying to live in that house. Amazing, Phil received a call to the First Baptist Church of San Clemente, California, and we moved into that very same model home!

Even more amazing, a friend bought our home in Chandler before it was placed on the market. God has always carefully provided for our family.

I asked the Lord to let my children grow up in one school system and have a place they would remember as home! And despite my fears of what life in California would entail, God protected our family and provided our children with stability. Our children all graduated from the same high school and still have many of the same friends.

Phil and I began praying about the next phase of life. He was given a special commendation for his 37 years in the Air Force Chaplaincy and served his last two-week active duty tour as a Chaplain in February of 1985.

His last assignment was at the Monterey Language Institute where over 4000 service members from all branches of the military were studying different languages: Russian was the biggest study group.

Looking back, we can see how God allowed Phil to have this assignment as preparation for our future ministry in Eastern Europe. Through the courtesy of the Slavic Gospel Association, Phil was able to deliver 200 Russian Bibles to the Russian professor, Alex

Holodilloff for distribution amongst the Russian professors on the faculty at the Defense Language Institute.

What a privilege to be able to make God's Word available! We discovered that the Defense Language Institute is a mission field here at home; on the faculty are Koreans, Chinese, Germans, Persians, Poles, Russians and many others!

CHAPTER THREE

Transition to Mission

Isaiah 45:5-6: "I will strengthen you; so that from the rising of the sun to the place of its setting, people may know that there is none beside me...
I am the Lord."

During our days at Turlock Baptist Church Phil wrote: "*One day while placing my collection of Bibles on a table, in preparation for a Missions conference, I was struck by the fact that I owned over 100 Bibles!*"

He had been reading the letters of Brother Andrew, and Corrie ten Boom, and others working in countries where Bibles and study materials were nearly nonexistent. He was deeply touched to learn that many communist governments prohibited Bibles to be printed or brought into their countries from the West. Giving money no longer felt like enough of a response to Phil, and he began to pray.

Additional communication came to him, telling of hundreds of secret camps and underground churches in Eastern Europe. It was reported that persecution only made the believers stronger and Phil thought this was something that our churches in the West needed to know more about.

His questions and research led to a phone call from a Mr. Newman who worked with Eastern European Bible Mission and wished to speak to both of us. That visit resulted in an invitation from Hank Paulson, the General Director of EEBM for us both to become a part of this ministry.

This was certainly not the kind of mission work we had ever thought about doing! We were not of Eastern European descent, nor did we know any of the languages, and as a pastor and military man we thought Phil might have difficulty entering those countries

However, the need to share with the Western church God's plan for reaching the whole world struck a chord in our hearts. Our kids were grown and out of the nest and we were free to trust God for this next step. Hank's letter to our church and to our friends and relatives explained:

August 1983

To the friends of Phil and Cindy Smith,

After more than twenty years of International and Pastoral experience, God has called Phil and Cindy to a new area of ministry.

Phil and Cindy will be personally involved in traveling and ministering to the needs of Christians in Eastern Europe – bringing them greetings from fellow believers in the West. They will bring Bibles and teaching aids, and will minister to them in person, as well as be learning much from our brothers and sisters in Eastern Europe.

They will live in the U.S. for most of the year, directing our ministry to the church in the U.S. Sharing the testimony, com-

mitment and strength of the Christians in Eastern Europe, they will encourage the church in the U.S. to become more personally involved in 'bearing one another's burdens'. (Galatians 6;2). Both Phil and Cindy would like to be able to share with you in a more personal way how God is leading in their lives and what their new ministry will entail.

We believe that the Lord will use them both in an important way to serve and strengthen His church, both in the U.S. and in Eastern Europe. As Phil and Cindy allow Christ to work through their lives, touching the lives of many in need, we encourage you to be a part of their ministry.

With Christian love and warm greetings from the Suffering Church,

Hank Paulson

We moved on Christmas day in 1983 to San Ramon, California and Phil began his work at the EEBM office in Walnut Creek. He was busy getting acquainted with the challenge before him and he loved it all.

Through some friends, we were introduced to the Presbyterian Church in Danville, California. Before long, I was sitting in on the Mission committee meetings and interviewing college students seeking funds for summer mission trips. Phil enjoyed the men's Bible study fellowship, and we were blessed that Pastor Orville Schick and his wife became our good friends.

The travels that we were to make that first summer were meant to be secret! But the last Sunday morning before we flew out for a summer in Eastern Europe, Pastor Orville had us stand and told the whole congregation what we were about to do and led the congregation in prayer. God gave us a body of people whom we grew to love and who supported us in many ways over the years.

CHAPTER FOUR

Behind The Wall

Psalm 119:105: "Your word is a lamp to my feet and a light for my path."

We had been invited to join a summer ministry group in Holland for the short training and an assignment somewhere 'beyond the wall'. First organized by Brother Andrew, the ministry was now housed at Hank Paulson's 'farm' in Holland where vehicles were customized for hiding Bibles, and summer missionaries were trained. The volunteers were all older believers who could spend a month or more in training and travel.

On arrival, we met Luise a secretary from the Eastern Europe Bible Mission and Patrick, our driver. When we arrived at the farm, we were given our schedule of training sessions and just a few days later we were given a 'road test' to see if we could help drive the vehicle in case Patrick became too weary!

Not allowed to see how they packed the vehicle for the trip, we only knew that it had been donated and then remodeled for the trip. It would only be used once for this country!

We were also to pull a small camping trailer and were not to travel on the big highways as our special cargo caused us to surpass the load limit of our vehicle. We would be taking smaller roads and stopping in Hungary first to off load the trailer and leave it behind at a camp ground for 10 days. We would pick it up on our way back to Holland.

An important part of our training was for each of us to memorize a portion of the route we were to take inside the 'closed countries' we would enter. I really wondered if I could remember all of it, but my early training as a child in the South Dakota prairie quickly came to mind. "Go so many fences, up a hill; turn right at the broken fence…"

The morning of our ministry trip came all too quickly and we were sent off with prayers and food and camping equipment neatly packed in our trunk. Our one small Bible was concealed inside the waist of my slacks. I thought I had given up tent camping after our kids were grown, but we had a tent with us as well!

We had special permission to spend the first night in a tiny pension at the top of a hill overlooking Hungary, but were shocked in the morning to find that one of the trailer tires was flat. Unfortunately we had no spare or any repair supplies since our cargo space was considered too precious and was filled with Bibles and literature.

I can honestly say that we did not panic, as we knew that our Lord was fully in charge of the situation. Patrick told us that delays were God's way of keeping us where He wanted us-until the right people were at the border patrol stations!

However, it was Sunday and we were in Austria, which is a Catholic nation: everyone was at church and all the gas stations and garages were closed!

Patrick walked to the church and asked some men leaving the worship service to help and sure enough, God had led him to two men who ran a garage! They had a tire that would fit our trailer, but they wanted Patrick to unload the trailer so it would be easier to jack up and replace the tire. There was no way we could risk our special cargo being discovered, so Patrick found several big husky Austrian men to hoist the trailer onto the jack. God was demonstrating His provision for our very first challenge!

Praising God, we began our journey to the first custom border station into Hungary. For the first time I saw those high towers on each side of the crossing with men pointing guns at us. Dogs were led around to sniff at our car and our gear. Dogs were barking in the 'no man's land' between the two borders and everyone around us seemed so sad and serious.

It seemed as though the officials were trying to act tough and show their authority. We noticed that the car ahead of us was searched thoroughly as the officials took off the inside of its doors.

When they came to our car we held our breath until they examined our Jiffy popcorn container: when they shook it they seemed amused! We were quickly waved on through to Hungary- God was again proving His provision of love and care for each step of our trip!

Traveling inside Hungary wasn't easy as there were no street signs! Patrick had made mental note of the campground he wanted to use and we soon found our way. At twilight, Patrick pulled on strings inside the camper and soon books, Bibles and literature came tumbling out! They were placed in black plastic bags in the trunk of our car and we took off for a visit.

A few miles down the road Patrick told us to pray because there was a police car following us. In order to travel safely as tourists, we were supposed to have special visas and we were not on a road leading to any tourist attraction. Instead we were driving a car full of Bible literature and food to bring to a pastor planning to lead a ministry camp in the mountains of Romania!

The police car continued to follow us, but a car with no lights on pulled out from a side road and nearly hit us. Swerving around us, the police stopped the other car and we were able to safely travel on the pastor's house!

Warmly greeted at the pastor's house and treated to tea and breads, we shared a short time of worship - what a precious time as we thanked the Lord for bringing us together and for the days in the mountains ahead of us.

Once it was dark we unloaded the 'goods' and watched as the Bibles were

hidden underneath the floor of the chicken coop! The pastor and his wife, Istvan and Uzonka, seemed delighted to meet us, telling us that they had never had a pastor and his wife our age visit before.

Saying goodbye to Istvan and Uzonka we drove back to the campground, pretending that we had been visiting a hangout for tourists in town. Patrick had to pay the gatekeeper to let us in and then we spent time gathering the things we would need for the next two weeks – we would leave the empty trailer in the campground while we were gone.

We were so grateful for the many ways God provided for us on this journey. Phil wrote to friends and supporters in the States to share his insights and to give thanks.

Dear Friends,

Although our border crossings took up to 4 hours to accomplish, we were amazed at the peace of God's presence and the smoothness with which we passed through inspections. We were extremely conscious of your prayers for us. Thank you so very much! We saw many miracles -God does work on behalf of his children!

We spent one week in a youth camp in the mountains with 30 young adults and 2 pastors who had gathered from several Eastern European countries. We had to move the camp 75 miles away to a remote cabin at one point to avoid the threat of exposure.

How I wish you could have heard the testimonies of these folks, and learn of the hardships and oppression they have endured because they follow Jesus. And I also wish you could see their hunger for the Word and the joy they have in sharing the scripture and the eagerness of the leaders to teach!

Two of the young men were seminary students from their nation's only approved seminary. A KGB agent lived on the seminary campus and called them in for 'interrogation' on a regular basis. Some complaints about this situation got out to the West and the KGB agent was moved off campus, yet is still present in the classes.

God is surely using the ministry of these faithful pastors and teachers. They are encouraged to see many coming to Christ, but they need Bibles and study materials!

Pray with me about how we can encourage them. They were so happy to see Cindy and me: We represent the love and prayers of Western believers! As our leader in Holland told us, "Just show up and it speaks volumes to the believers that they are not forgotten by the West…that you really do pray for them and would risk your lives to encourage them with your visit" It is a joy and privilege to be here at this time in history.

Yours in Christ,

Phil

Early the next morning we paid our rent for the space and set off to camp in the mountains of Romania -.but first another border crossing!

Istvan and Uzonka

Phil and I were blessed to meet so many wonderful people throughout Eastern Europe. We learned so much about trusting God from these saints who prevailed in hard times - quiet unassuming people who had a tremendous impact. When we first met Istvan and Uzonka Boytor, they were simply a stop along the way to another destination. But soon they were so much more than a stop – they had a tremendous impact on our understanding of how faithful God's people were in difficult circumstances.

Listen to how Hank and Mona Paulson describe this couple in September 1994.

There is situated in Northeastern Hungary, a little hamlet, Fony, which is unadvertised and unknown to tourists. Budapest, the metropolitan capital city, is the attraction for Western tourists — yet the region around Fony has been a spiritual hotbed for 400 years!

In 1554, the first Bible in the Hungarian language was translated and printed here. Three hundred years later a new young minister and his bride were allowed to pastor a church in this obscure place by the Communist government. The regime thought they had solved the 'problem' of this dynamic man of faith and his tenacious commitment to Christ. They placed him in isolation so he wouldn't bother them or anyone else. How their plan backfired!

Now, more than a generation later, Istvan Boytor and his wife, Uzonka, are still producing fruit for God's Kingdom. Istvan and Uzonka arise with the crowing rooster at 5:00 a.m. to get the show on the road: the show being 13 weeks of summer camps.

Through all those years, Istvan and Uzonka were committed to bloom where they were planted. They started reaching out to the local teenagers in a parsonage with no indoor plumbing. Besides being head pastor of their village church, they had a dynamic youth ministry for the young people who were fed up with Communist lies and wanted truth. It was bad for the government and even Istvan's church supervisor who had not expected a vital ministry.

Despite opposition, intimidation and threats, Istvan and Uzonka kept up their outreach. Decades ago, they sponsored youth camps held secretly in the mountains in Romania and Poland. They discipled young people and counseled them about marriage and having an uncompromising walk with Christ. These young people, now grown, are scattered across Slovakia, Hungary and Romania as spiritual leaders.....blooming where they are planted.

After the secret camp in Romania (which you'll hear about in the next chapter), was over, we returned to the house while Istvan stayed behind in the mountains for more camps. We brought back some of the camping supplies and gave a report to Uzonka when I noticed that she was limping and discovered that her shoe was badly torn. I got a piece of paper and traced her feet for a pattern so that shoes could be purchased for her back in Holland. The next team coming to Romania delivered new shoes to her.

Thank you Father for these faithful Saints that you have placed all over your world… and thank you for the sustaining grace and wisdom you give them to carry on faithfully.

CHAPTER FIVE

Heading to Romania

Psalm 121:7-8: "The Lord will keep you from all harm –he will watch over your life; the Lord will watch over your coming and going both now and forevermore."

The Romanian border crossing was much more secure, with more police and dogs, more towers and men with binoculars and guns! Back in Holland I had been given an English magazine – I was meant to sit quietly in the front seat and read with my sunglasses on.

It felt like being in a play! As the guards strode past our car with their dogs, I prayed for each one to learn of the freedom they could have in Christ. Despite the fact that their guns were pointed at us, they were the ones imprisoned!

We waited for several hours before being allowed to proceed through the 'no man's land' filled with mines and barbed wire and dogs- I could never understand why they went to such trouble to keep folks in Romania when they constantly shouted over loud-speakers in the village what a wonderful leader they had and how great he was treating them.

Before I tell you about our time in Romania, listen to Phil's experience, in his own words about one of the many "humorous" experiences he had at the border - taken from his journal:

I had to be rebuked today - I was sitting in the car at that first border, it was hot and smelly. There were so many pesky flies and I was swatting them when Patrick (our driver) looked over and asked me to sit quietly. He suggested that I just keep reading my magazine, saying that flies don't bother these people!

I looked up and said, "Why do you think God made flies?"

Immediately I knew I was in trouble – I was speaking in English at the border, with all kinds of police walking about, and listening devices in the trees. I was supposed to be calm and act as though I do this every day!

Patrick gave me a very disgusted look! Ouch Lord, I am so sorry. I do not want to cause this dear young man any more stress than he already has, taking two old folks to a place they have never been before!

As if that wasn't bad enough, I grew amused at all the little cars in line at the border and began to sing a little song that started in my head (one little, two little, three little Fiats, four little, five little six little Fiats…) and then somehow came out of my mouth. Patrick and Cindy both shot me a look and I learned that my songs are not appreciated, especially at border crossings.

On the Road Again

Now it was finally my turn to remember where to go next. I knew we needed to drive several miles on the first dirt road to the left to a clearing where cars would be parked against the trees. We would meet someone there who would lead us further up the mountain. But first we would sleep in our car overnight.

Suddenly we saw men waving at us and motioning us off the dirt road into some trees. Back in the brush we saw half a dozen cars and some men and women coming out to meet us. Soon we were all hugging and whispering. No one spoke English but it didn't matter: we were where we needed to be!

The folks in the cars shared some berries and bread with us and we gave them some hard sausage we had brought from Austria. Somehow we managed to sleep a few hours until a rap on the window woke us so we could hurry into the bushes to go to the bathroom and get back on the road.

After several hours of travel, one car ahead of us motioned for us to pull off to the side of the road and wait for a signal to continue. The rest of the route needed to be checked, and we were happy to have a chance to get out of the car and toss our Frisbee. We noticed some young children watching us and we had fun teaching them how to throw a Frisbee! Then the signal to leave came and we had to take our Frisbee away from one little boy and make a dash to the car. I felt guilty about taking a toy away from a child, but I knew he might have a difficult time explaining to his parents about us!

The next day the pastor at camp told me that the children we had met belonged to the state of Romania. Their fathers were soldiers and their mothers were sheepherders or prostitutes and they had been produced to be slaves of the state, to herd sheep. I was in shock!

As we approached the mountain we would hike over to get to camp, we backed our car into the brush to conceal the license plate from Holland. Others came down to help carry the supplies we had brought, and as we approached the ridge of the mountain we heard singing. A group of young adults were singing a Welcome Song for us!

The folks at the secret camp had gathered from several countries for a once in a lifetime experience. Some had come on buses, while others hiked most of the way, with only the clothes on their backs and the food they could carry in backpacks. The food was pooled and we all took turns deciding how to use it.

I was so impressed by the desire of the young adults to copy scripture passages – none but the pastors had a copy of the Bible. Some had pages torn from a Bible and some had passages they had copied.

Campfires could only be lit in the daytime – we had to keep our location secret! But in the evening as we crept into our little tent we could hear them singing a chorus or songs we had taught them that day. At times we could hear campers reciting passages of scripture!

The days were filled with Bible studies, questions and lots of prayer! Often we would not know what was going on but we prayed as these precious folks poured out their hearts to the pastors and their fellow campers.

During our time at camp I met a woman named Elizabeth who

became my friend. She could speak some English and she taught me to shower in a waterfall by putting your head in first to numb your body - the women went up stream to bathe while the men went downstream!

One day Elizabeth asked if she could have a private conversation with me. She wanted to tell me about a decision she needed to make; about whether she should get married. As a pharmacist she was able to keep her family supplied with the medications they needed. Her mother was 'dangerously' ill she said.

Her father was the one older man at the camp and her brother was one of the pastors. She told me that her brother's church was growing and the government was about to put him into prison. When he went to prison she would need to provide for his wife and children as well as her parents. Her heartbreaking question was… "Why did God give me the desire to be this man's wife -to love him and have his children if I am needed by my family?

She asked for wisdom to understand the ways of God, telling me that she already knew what she was supposed to do, but wondered why God would make her feel passion for someone He did not want her to have! We prayed and asked God to show her the answer that He wanted her to find and to be able to accept it and live joyously in His will.

I told her that, with her permission, I would share her story with my friends and we would pray for her. She was thrilled to think that her needs would be shared with people in America!

For years I shared her story…and not until rather recently did

I hear that her brother did not go to prison and she did indeed marry that man!

Near the end of the camp session a shepherd found us as he came up the hill. He wanted money to keep our secret, and after he left, the pastors decided that we should move the camp to another part of the mountain.

After a long drive we arrived at a new meeting place, an old cabin that was more like a barn. We lost nearly half of the group during the move, but gained a few new people. I still cannot fathom how the people communicated with one another without any phones!

Patrick told us that we would be leaving soon to drive to the farthest border of Romania to take a message to a doctor planning to conduct another secret camp the following week. His camp plans had been discovered and we were to warn him not to meet!

We would only have Sunday to drive the many miles, check out the suggested route to get to the doctor's home, deliver the message on Monday and then drive all the way back across Romania before our visa expired on Wednesday. We would have only one day to pick up our trailer in Hungary before our papers expired for that visit too!

So off to the border town of Lasi, Romania we went. Lasi was a training camp

for border guard soldiers. When we arrived Sunday, Patrick told us to look to our right and get a glimpse of the front gate of the Camp. Our 'friends' lived in the back of this camp.

The believers had often been persecuted and the Border training camp had extended its walls to surround their home! To gain entry we would walk straight through the gates, dressed like locals. Patrick would go before us and turn an outside light on and leave a gate ajar for us at the safe house.

On Monday morning, we took care to communicate through scribbled notes, while chatting out loud about sightseeing plans. We did not know that on Monday all the museums and other tourist sites were closed! We ended up walking through the parks, with a man with a camera following us. We ended up agreeing to split up and meet back at the hotel.

I headed to the meager shopping center and looked around a bit, but because I did not have the proper papers I could not buy anything. Eventually I returned to the hotel through the bar.

Phil had the police following him the entire time, possibly thinking that as he was the eldest, he must be the leader! When he rejoined me and Patrick we laughed about our adventure and then pulled out our darkest clothes for the evening.

After dinner at a nice restaurant we strolled to a park where music was playing. We knew it was a straight shot - about a mile to the camp. Patrick and I had walked that way earlier in the day, hoping to find another entrance. Unfortunately, behind the Border Guard Camp was a steep hill covered with broken glass which would be unsafe after dark. In the front gate we must go!

As it grew darker Patrick left us sitting on a bench near the entrance to a park, praying silently. Phil had removed his eyeglasses and his watch because older men in Romania did not wear them. After an hour or so, since Patrick had not returned, we set out for the front gate.

When a city bus pulled up in front of the gate we slipped into the crowd and went through the first gate, not looking at the guard in his tower. Keeping to our left, we headed towards the back, passing another tower, whose guard had come down to flirt with some young women.

We quietly walked past, as though we did this every night of our lives. All of a sudden there were bright lights and a policeman and some men working on a hole in the ground. Just past the lights we could see a gate open and a house light on. Walking quietly around the men, we went into the open gate and on into the house without knocking. We had not been given these instructions, but the Lord led us step by step, providing an open path.

Inside the doorway, we heard a tape of children singing gospel songs so we knew we were in the right place. A woman in the hallway was startled when she saw us, but she motioned for us not to talk, but to follow her.

In the next room we found Patrick and some members of the household who just happened to come out of the mountains that afternoon to visit Maria! They were English teachers who had never met English speakers before and were delighted to talk with us.

Maria called her son, the doctor, who was on his way in his medical van. When he arrived he told us the story of how his father had been killed for his faith and how many times the government had tried to persecute him, his mother and recently his brother! He was sad to have to cancel camp, but grateful not to endanger his friends.

After worshipping with them, I realized that we needed to leave and I had not practiced in my mind, the steps to get out of the compound. Our orders from Holland were to never be seen in a vehicle with any of these believers, but the young doctor turned to me wanting to drive us back to the city center.

We of course told him no, but as he looked at me, he must have seen that my heart was saying......*help!* He stood up and said...."It is final! I will take you." He told us to give him a few minutes to prepare his vehicle and to slide into the van with heads down and stay on the floor until we arrived at a safe place.

At a park, near our hotel, we exited the medical van and hugged and prayed with him. We spoke of meeting again in Eternity....a place very real to him.

At the hotel we went into the Bar entrance, pretending we had been there all evening! Then we went up the stairs to our room and prepared our things to leave in the morning. We made a hasty trip back to the border of Hungary, and then on to Austria where we checked into a nice pension and slept for a day.

Back in Holland we were given our next assignment - to take a Mission van to Poland for a Family Camp. We were to drive across East Germany, which was known for its police harassment....but before I tell you about that, listen to Phil's excitement about our trip to Romania in a letter he wrote to friends and family upon our return:

Dear Friends,

We are just back from our first trip to Romania, and have been told that next we will be driving a large van to Poland, taking along a music leader named Joan. We will be the guest speakers at a two-week family camp to be held in the countryside. Our main topic is to be about Christian Marriage, and this is all we know!

No one from our mission has been there before so we do not know what the security issues will be. Our cover story is that we are tourists camping and sightseeing in Poland. We are getting our visa papers and will leave next week.

We need your prayers!"

We have boxes of Dutch food to eat during the 3-4 days it will take to reach our destination, but how do we read the Dutch instructions? We also have names and places to memorize. We can carry a Bible for each of us and I can take my notes in my black notebook. We are finishing our preparations by taking turns practicing our van driving skills!

"We plan to be gone for three weeks on this trip. Thanks for praying!"

Phil

CHAPTER SIX

Off to Poland

Psalm 84:11: "For the Lord is a sun and shield; the Lord bestows favor and honor; no good thing does he withhold from those whose walk is blameless."

The reunion with the team in Holland was sweet. Patrick gave the report at the Sunday night gathering, and when one director asked me (when I was barely out of the car), "Tell me would you do it again?" I answered that I would but would like a bath first!

Half the Fun is Getting There

Several women's groups in America had given me a suitcase full of fabric, thread, needles and even a big pile of squares of bright fabric, to use for quilts. Since we had room in the van we packed it along with small bars of soap, shampoo and toothpaste. And this time we made sure to bring some road repair equipment! Poland would be our next big adventure.

Along the way we got lost or mixed up several times when we entered cities. A sign would read this way to the Centrum (city center) with an arrow, and then another sign would instruct you to go in the opposite direction! We found ourselves going in circles!

Once while we were hopelessly lost, a motorcycle cop pulled up beside us and looked at our map, seeing where we wanted to go. He beckoned for us to follow, and I reached in my bag and handed him a candy bar. He smiled broadly and took us safely to the road we needed to reach our destination.

Smiling again, he waved his candy bar and zoomed away.

Later when we told this story to the campers, they told us that Poland did not have motorcycle officers at that time, and especially not in the city! Phil laughed and said he had fun giving a candy bar to an angel!

We arrived to find the camp was being held in a country farm house and a group of cabins. Some families were just getting settled, while others had been there for a week. This type of camping group would appear to be a common sight as families often vacationed together and businesses arranged for vacation spots out in the country for their people.

Although we did not have official permission to meet with the Polish people, there was not the degree of secrecy which we experienced in Romania. A visitor from Holland the previous year had met this pastor, and this is how we were invited.

The very first thing the pastor said to us (even before hello) was that "there will be no women wearing makeup. (Luckily I had long left makeup back in the States,) "No women will wear jewelry or revealing clothes like shorts."

We certainly got the message that he was not too happy about having two women in this teaching team! He went on to say,'No women can preach or teach.' As graciously as we could, we agreed to his very clear conditions, and then he seemed to warm up a bit.

When Phil asked about when and for how long he should expect to speak, the pastor answered that Phil could speak that night and the pastor would decide later if he would be allowed to speak again! We thanked him and noticed that out of all the men at camp, the pastor was the only one dressed formally in a dark suit and tie.

Unfortunately when Phil began to unload the van, he discovered that his suitcase with his suit and ties had been left in Holland: it was a very tense evening for Phil! After explaining to the pastor, Phil borrowed a roomy blue sweater of mine and looked very nice. The group loved the musician we had brought along, and I just smiled a lot.

Phil must have passed the test, as he was asked to teach many times a day, until one day the Pastor suggested that they all go to the nearby lake for a day of fun. Phil reported that at the lake the women swam in their underwear! So much for Pastor's modesty rules!

I decided to pull out my fabric squares and give them to women. Back in the States someone had obviously spent a lot of time carefully arranging these blocks, with matching colors to make a beautiful design. But when I distributed them, the first thing the ladies did, was to break apart the piles and mix them up the way they wished. It was truly a cultural adaption of design.

Many of the women remembered their grandmothers making

bedspreads with scraps of old clothes. However, today in 1983, they had to stand in line and use coupons from the government to get clothes or fabric. Even needles and thread are very hard to get! How happy they were that I had a needle for each woman!

Between the teaching sessions, we sat and began sewing our little pile of blocks

together. Several women worked to make a bigger piece and before you know it we had a cot size quilted blanket top pulled together. We decided to give it to the pastor's wife, as she had many guests at their home. She spent so many hours cooking for the camp that I hardly saw her.

I was praying for a way to finish off this little blanket, when a request came for us to drive our translator and his wife to their hometown. He had a phone call telling him that his mother was dying and that there had been a bad flood in southern Poland. He needed to check on his parents and we had the only available transportation. Phil and I left with the translator and his wife and baby to spend the weekend with his family and speak in their church on Sunday.

We felt blessed to be in their little house church, but were sad to discover that the mother of the translator was seriously ill. We wondered if Pavel would be able to return to the Camp with us. His wife and baby stayed with his family, but Pavel returned with us, committed to finish the work at camp.

On our way back I told Pavel that I needed to buy a blanket to be the filling for the quilt, as well as a large piece of fabric for the bottom layer. Dropping me off at one store, he took Phil to another store to see if they could purchase some underwear and socks.

When he came back to see how I was doing, folks were staring at me and laughing as I was trying to point to the fabric which I wanted to buy. I was not making much headway! Pavel was able to conclude the deal and I happily got my fabric and blanket.

When I asked why the people were laughing, Pavel told me that I had been in the line for engaged couples to get fabric for their first home and I did not have any proper ration coupons. He said they decided to help me when he told them that I was teaching Polish women how to tear up fabric, and then sew it together to make a blanket! They seemed to think it was a very funny idea.

Back at camp, the women were ecstatic to see the pretty fabric I bought and they worked diligently to finish the quilt. Our translator asked if I would like to speak to the women and so I began teaching about women in the Bible and how Jesus used women to do his work. We had discussions about how these stories impacted their life today and I asked them to share Bible stories like this with other women. This is not common practice in this church in Poland at this time: women have only men teachers. Praise the Lord for a beginning!

When we left that camp we noticed that the pastor was not wearing a tie anymore, and seemed to be relaxed, enjoying his people and his time with them. He cried when we said goodbye and invited us to come next summer, asking if I would teach the women. He also asked for a copy of my notes! I gave him the questions I used and Bible references, and also knew that each of these Bible lectures had been recorded for later use.

Back in Holland, we turned in the van, gave our reports and prepared for the busy trip back home. Our assignment was to cross the USA speaking on behalf of the mission, beginning in Philadelphia. We would be 6 months on the road sharing in small meetings, and one on one with individuals. Because our Eastern European mission is underground, we even had to be careful in the United States in how we were announced or advertised so as not to draw attention to secret churches.

Listen to Phil's heart from this journal entry from August of 1984. God was continuing to grow his heart for missions:

Praise the Lord for six months of serving the Lord with the Eastern European Bible Mission: It has been a period of learning the needs of the body of Christ in this part of the world. The more I am immersed in this work the more I want to serve!

Cindy joined me in February for my last two week tour as an Air Force Chaplain. In October, I will retire from the Reserves after 32 years. My last assignment, my favorite, has been serving the 4000 men and women studying 47 different languages at the Defense Language Institute at the Presidio of Monterey, California. What an exciting 'spare time' ministry this has been.

God, in His infinite wisdom, allowed me to have this assignment as a preparation for our ministry with EEBM. Recently I met a Christian Russian professor, and through the kindness of the Slavic Gospel Association I was able to give him 200 Rus-

sian Bibles to distribute to the Russian professors on the faculty of the Defense Language Institute. We both rejoiced greatly over this privilege of making God's word available. This place is a mission field here right at home!

Pray for the believers here as they continue to witness for Christ.

Cindy and I are preparing for another trip to Holland and Eastern Europe,

knowing of only one assignment to an adult camping ministry in Poland. Godly marriage is the suggested curriculum for a 15 day camp with couples. Please pray for us and this particular ministry.

We expect to be visiting churches and encouraging pastors and leaders. We will not only put together a list of practical needs, but are also seeking teaching and training tools to better equip the precious people we will meet.

Returning to the USA in September, we will once again cross the country to share our stories. We thank you for your prayers and personal support for us as we continue to seek God's will in this exciting ministry.

CHAPTER SEVEN

Sharing Across America

Proverbs 25:12: "Who is the man who fears the Lord? He will instruct him in the way he should choose."

To say we were excited to share about our experiences back home would be a drastic understatement. In one letter Phil wrote,

> *What a thrilling year 1983-84 was for us! Praise the Lord for His abundant mercy and grace as we traveled into Eastern Europe and ministered in Hungary, Romania and Poland! We enjoyed meeting the believers in these countries, and observing their victorious faith. It has made an indelible impression on our lives.*

We both wished every pastor in America could have the privilege of being with the Christians in Eastern Europe for at least one month. We were convinced that renewal would happen in churches if leaders could experience what we had experienced. We were determined to get the word out.

As we drove across our great country and visited churches from California to Massachusetts, we were encouraged to see so many Christians who were excited about what God is doing throughout the world.

Phil wrote,

> *"We felt a fresh breeze of spiritual awakening all across America and sensed the Spirit working in churches of all kinds. We saw God at work in our United States Air Force Academy and learned of His work in Washington, D.C. in the lives of high officials and government leaders. We are excited by the desire of others to learn what God is doing in Eastern Europe."*

We always loved hearing how God worked when we spoke or shared about our ministry, whether it is in Eastern Europe, or the United States. A young man from Dallas wrote to us;

> *"God bless you! I would like to thank you for sharing with us at my church. I have committed to pray for you and EEBM at least three times a week for the next year. Thank you for obeying the call of the Lord and going where so many others can't or won't go. You encourage me!"*

And then, while in Colorado, Phil shared at a church mission conference about his embarrassing experience of arriving at a family camp in Poland, only to realize that he had left his suitcase behind. He had to ask his translator to go with him to the nearest town to buy some underwear and socks, only to spend two afternoons searching stores with empty shelves.

After hearing that story, a nine-year old boy was so touched that he brought us a bag of his socks, to take to the children of Poland. He and his friends later gave me $1.45 to buy a treat for the children at the upcoming summer camp to which we would be returning!

In addition to speaking across the country, Phil continued to write words of gratitude to our growing list of supporters. Here's an example of a letter Phil wrote that summer (this also will give you a feel for what we shared in person):

Dear Friends and Family,

This month we received a touching letter from a pastor in Poland who was also at the family camp last summer. He writes in English:

"I want you to know that very often I come back in my thinking to the blessed time that we spent together. It would be really wonderful to meet you again and praise the Lord together."

We are so grateful to the Lord for you. Without the prayers, encouragement and financial help of you who 'stand by the stuff' (I Sam. 30:24) we could not have this ministry to the body of Christ in these lands behind the Iron Curtain. You are our partners and co-laborers for Christ. We need each other. You are the supply line! I think of the responsive faces of those I met this past summer; they were so eager to learn Biblical truth, and hungry for teaching on godly marriage and a personal walk with Christ.

Just now there is an opening in parts of Eastern Europe- the churches who have been meeting in secret in the forests are so excited about the ability to meet in summer camps for weeks at a time. We must respond while the doors are opening. The living conditions are very poor but the desire to be free and to begin anew is very strong. We hear one request over and over: "Please tell the believers in America to pray for us"

These are exciting days and so many need Christ: we need to be prepared!

In the next weeks we leave for Hawaii to meet with a couple

who have made one trip to Eastern Europe and have invited
us to come and share in several places. They are praying about
returning to teach in Romania once again.

Afterwards we will travel across the States to visit our children
and their families and then travel from the East Coast to Ger-
many and then on by train to our base camp in Holland.

Please pray for physical, mental and spiritual preparation for
each of these places in which the Lord is leading us to minis-
ter-.here and over there!

Pray for capable and dedicated translators. Pray for the gift of
spiritual discernment as we help pastors lead in challenging sit-
uations. Pray for a young couple to accompany us to lead youth
and children's meetings.

Again, thank you for being a part of what God is doing
around the World!

Praising Him,

Phil Smith

Our Time in Hawaii:

We had a wonderful two and a half weeks sharing the good news
of God's work in Eastern Europe in Hawaii. Bob and Norma
Owens were our coordinators in Honolulu and have ministered in
Eastern Europe and have a real heart for the church there. Listen
to Phil's description of our trip:

In Honolulu we not only spoke in services at Bob's church but
also at the Christian Medical Association, the Ministerial
Association, a chapel service at International College, and in

several churches and evangelical groups. We were even inter-viewed on 4 radio stations and a TV station talk show. (Our faces were blocked out). In each place we saw the Lord visibly touching lives in different ways.

On the North Shore of Oahu we were invited to share in the evening service of the North Shore Christian Fellowship, which reaches many surfers for Christ.

At the close of one service, a young man approached Cindy and said, "I was fascinated by what you said, but I don't know why I am here. In fact, I don't even remember how I got here!"

Cindy said; "maybe you are here because you need the Lord". When he answered saying maybe that was true, Cindy asked one of the Elders to talk with him. Later he approached Cindy and told her that he had accepted Christ as his Savior that night. As it turned out he was a well-known surfer and many had been praying for his salvation.

In this same service three young men came to me at the close of my talk. All three were U.S. servicemen; one was Army, one was Air Force, and one was Navy! The Navy man was a big, husky, Russian Jew who spoke to me with much fervor. "I am a completed Jew," he said, "God spoke to me tonight and I want to go to Eastern Europe-. God wants me there to serve Him!" Each of these men had a fascinating story to tell of their deter-mination to serve the Lord. My how that service inspired me!

God is good! As we wrapped up our time sharing across the states, we began to prepare for our next adventures in Europe. .

CHAPTER EIGHT

Seeing God's Hand

Psalm 127:1-2: "Unless the Lord builds the house, its builders labor in vain. Unless the Lord watches over the city, the watchmen stand guard in vain.

I wrote the following while in Poland:

> *We are in Poland with Phil teaching families about biblical marriage and walking in Christ. I take notes, recording the questions that are asked and the answers Phil gives. It seems that the Pastor here is asking the most questions and so I am not too surprised when he asks me afterwards for a copy of my notes.*

> *Even after Phil offers him a copy of his teaching notes, the pastor still wants my comments! So we leave behind my notes, even though they are written in English. We are told the pastor will study them with help from the translator. We are reminded again of their immense hunger for biblical teaching.*

> *Pavel, our translator, tells us that the most rapidly growing group of believers is the young people. Camps and other training sessions held throughout the year are building strong young leaders. He took us to the resort town, Wisla, which Pavel thinks could be used for year round outreach as it offers winter skiing and can be reached by train.*

Pavel shared that some have united with the Catholic Church and are forming a charismatic movement in Poland and while he can work with all the groups, his heart is with this pastor because of his steady teaching of the Word. We have been touched as we visit many of these churches and hear the_ believers pray. Without hesitation, they pray out loud, confessing their sins publicly.

It seems that the more you learn, the more there is to learn. One thing is for certain: God is at work here behind the Iron Curtain. Living here is a big challenge, but these are happy people, rejoicing and encouraging one another.

On Sunday as we drive to worship we see lines of people waiting to enter the Catholic Church. There is truly a hunger for God! We know that on Sunday afternoons, across the plowed fields, believers gather, hungry for worship and prayer. This is the church at worship in secret.

After the last session here in Poland, we are ready to leave, but first we enjoy the main meal of the day and then a final session with the pastor, over coffee. He began by apologizing for the primitive conditions of our housing, although I liked being out in the small farm setting! Next he told us how pleased he and his wife were with the women's sessions and how I am to take word back to Holland that these must continue! He also wants me to make sure to thank the Danville church for the craft supplies that the women used to make the quilt.

He wants a commitment that we will return next summer, but we can say only that we will follow what God has planned, although we would enjoy further partnership with him and his flock. This pastor is struggling so much, with resistance from both the government and his denomination, being criticized for inviting guests from the West to his fellowship.

Later the pastor gave us a list of what is needed for another camp to take place - these needs are representative of what is difficult to buy in Poland, due to rationing:

Sugar, butter, jam, chocolate, canned fish (tuna), meat, black pepper, canned tomatoes, salami, powdered milk, canned milk, and most of all toilet paper!

More tents are needed, as well as one large enough to seat 150 people and many teaching tapes and videos for children and young people are wanted.

Our translator chimed in with his list of a study Bible, and teaching tapes, as well as some help understanding the cults now sending materials into Poland - he asked for teaching on 'How to discern the cults."

We enjoyed our last worship service, listening to the children sing song after song - the Polish people love music! At a camp-fire we were treated to roasted kielbasa and tiny apples on sticks! It was a bit like our American tradition of S'mores where we roast marshmallows and eat them on graham crackers!

After some tears when the pastor hugged Phil and they said goodbye, we were given a jug of sterile water and some sand-wiches and we were off.

We reached the border at dusk and exchanged our zloty (mon-ies). We found a simple place to spend the night and in the morning travelled through heavy rain through the DDR. After some difficulty finding our way through Berlin we waited for 35 minutes at the East German / West German border.

We travelled for almost 4 hours more to get to Helmstadt, where we found a clean old hotel downtown that had hot *water! It felt so wonderful and only cost us $21 for the night. Breakfast was wonderful; Eggs, cold meat, cheese, jam, butter, fresh bread and strong coffee!*

Finally on Sunday we made our final push toward Holland where we would be traveling on the autobahn. We called Holland to report that the "old folks were on their way back home!" We had strict orders to give a phone call report from West Germany!

Once we decided we had enough of autobahn food, we took a little road off to find a village with a restaurant, but all we could find was an ice cream shop - so we had coffee, ice cream and chocolates for dinner - not so healthy!

Stopping in a town south of Hannover for the night we walked around the narrow streets and peered into the dark shops and decided to spend a bit of time the next day shopping. Phil wanted another harmonica as he had given his away. After our shopping and a final great German meal, we headed back to the Base camp in Holland.

The Following Week in Holland:

We had given our reports, cleaned up the van and were making plans to visit Vienna to learn about the new underground seminary being organized by our mission. As our room at the 'farm' was needed for the next guests, we packed everything into storage where it would stay until we collected it on our way back to America.

We had a 14 hour train ride ahead of us which taught us to always travel first class by train in Europe. You get what you pay for! Our train ride cost us $300 for the sleeper, but we saved money by taking our own food.

We enjoyed a delightful retreat at the Rosenhof Guest House in Salzburg. We shared a bath with other guests, but the rooms were cozy and we enjoyed being called to meals by the sound of a little bell ringing!

On to Vienna:

Once in Vienna we were met by friends of friends and stayed in someone else's vacant apartment while they were on furlough. This is how it goes as you travel about: all contacts are important! We moved on to a pension for a few nights and then to another apartment made available for us. One surely learns to be portable, but in all the stops we caught a glimpse of a different housing situation in a different part of the city.

We had lots of fun with our friends, Hans and Donna and their children, Mark and Jeremy and enjoyed meeting with an associate of Brother Andrew, who shared with us about the ministries they were involved with in Eastern Europe.

After the International Church service we met the pastor and others at a McDonald's downtown. While I was speaking with Hans, he asked me what our future with EEBM looked like. I told him that we knew the mission was in transition and moving headquarters to Colorado but we would not be moving from California. We were waiting on the Lord for His will!

Hans was excited, telling me that they needed a pastor in their new ministry in BEE. BEE was Biblical Education by Extension, a traveling staff seminary, working secretly in several nearby countries to train pastors. If we were interested he wanted us to visit the office and meet the staff. Coincidentally, Jody and Linda Dillow, the present leaders of BEE, were in the restaurant!

Hans ushered us across the restaurant to meet Jody and Linda. If I thought Hans was eager for us to join them, I was not prepared for the eagerness of Jody!

They invited us to the 'house on the hill', which was secret to visitors. At first I was not that impressed as the house seemed big and empty and the few girls working there did not seem very friendly. Only the Art department was warm and exciting and we were interested to see how materials were being written, adapted, and translated with various cultural needs in consideration.

Jody was a persuasive sale person, telling us that he would prepare a job description for us and could see us doing hospitality as well as teaching out in the field. We told him we would pray about it and perhaps present it to Hank.

Back in Holland, when Hank asked us about our visit to BEE, Phil told him about the job opportunity and asked if Hank would send him to BEE. Hank told us no, as there was another staff person ahead of us who wanted that job. Hank needed us right where we were, and wanted Phil to write materials for the pastors that we would meet each summer.

Phil had difficulty not being a part of BEE just then! Back home in Danville, he began sharing with his men's group who had consistently encouraged and supported us all the time we were in ministry in Vienna.

It all begins with prayer! How many times have I reminded myself of this fact!

Praying with people who really know you.....with people who are not afraid to tell you what you need to do in your personal life first…

Praying for God's perfect timing in the place, the situation, the people and the funds…

A year of prayer and fasting passed and Phil decided to write up his resignation from EEBM and present it to the leadership. He had the letter in his pocket at a group conference when the director asked to speak to both Phil and me. He told us that he had no peace about saying no to us about working with BEE and asked if we were still interested. We said yes, and Phil quietly tore up that letter later than night!

I have thought about this situation many times - waiting is a huge part of God's working in our lives! We knew for certain this big step was of Him and now we needed to ask permission from our kids and their families to step even further out of their lives and of course we needed to raise the support to move to Vienna. These were secret ministries and we could not write or speak freely.

Our children supported our announcement. One said… "No surprise, we knew you would do this if you could". The men's group from Danville, with the encouragement and support of the pastor had us on our way in 3 months!

They were a valued support team during our years in Eastern Europe and later during our ministry in Vietnam. They sent videos of church services, they visited us on site, sometimes even sending ministry teams to come and work alongside us. One couple refurbished my office in Vienna. Others traveled alongside us, and brought the message seen and heard, home to their churches.

Even now I am strengthened and encouraged by the support of these folks—I now understand the love that the Apostle Paul had for his saints who loved and supported and worked alongside him. God gives us His encouragers along the way. I pray these words will bless you as you strengthen God's servants, whom God has placed in your path.

CHAPTER NINE

At Home in Austria

Proverbs 24:3-4: "By wisdom a house is built, and by understanding it is established; and by knowledge the rooms are filled with all precious and pleasant riches."

Austria served as our home base for our many journeys throughout Europe at this point in our lives.

Moving to Vienna, God blessed us by leading us to a temporary home whose owners (also working with our Mission) were on holiday. Our new neighbor, Heidi immediately befriended us and began teaching us how to find the best rental in Vienna.

We were introduced to a landlord who had built an apartment house and was renting out the apartment in which he had been living prior to getting married. We had a modern two bedroom apartment with a tiny kitchen, but a large balcony which held our small freezer. Soon it was covered with snow.

In the summers we would eat lunch or tend flowers and watch tourist buses driving up the street to visit a mountain village called Grinzing. I would see folks taking pictures of our quaint little balcony and flowers!

We arrived in October and Phil began teaching almost immediately. On his first trip to Romania he left wearing a light jacket and ball cap, as the fall weather was beautiful. Then a big snow storm swept in and he returned in a Russian style fur hat and a warm jacket. It seems some of the men in his class were happy to trade clothes with him.

Meanwhile I had the first of many new experiences. After attending church with me, several of the young people from our office left for another event. They had directed me as I drove to the church, so when I left alone, I wasn't quite sure how to make my way home. As I stepped out of the church, it was late afternoon and snow was falling. It was not easy to find the streets. My heart pleaded to the Father to get me home.

Soon I saw a snow plow coming in my direction, flashing his lights with the message that I needed to get out of the way. Backing into a driveway I watched him plow past me only to find that I was blocked in. I struggled and prayed, remembering snow banks in my early driving experience in South Dakota. Finally, I was out of the snow bank and on my way, guessing which road to take at each fork of the road. At last, I reached home and parked across the street. In the morning I could not even see the car under all the snow!

Phoning the office the next morning to tell them I would be late, I shocked the Austrian lady employed by our mission. She told me it was a snow holiday, as the first big storm of the season usually made it impossible for people to get around. It was best for me to stay put and let the government snow plows do their job! (Something I never heard in South Dakota).

One of the things we enjoyed most about our home in Sandgasse was the heated tiles in the floor. We often invited the staff over on the Friday nights that we were in town, because they loved visiting our warm apartment. Many lived in big, old houses where heating was YOU shoveling the coal into a furnace.

At first our neighbors in the building were very proper and did not speak with us or even make eye contact. We had to be very cautious about how we introduced ourselves as our ministry was 'underground' and we often explained that we were working with a publishing house. Slowly our neighbors began to care for us. One neighbor, spent many hours studying the Drivers license manual with me, in English and in German. The license testing was conducted in German. Another neighbor brought us lovely gifts of china and porcelain. They loved to hear of our funny experiences adjusting to their culture.

One young neighbor, from a Muslim background, was working in the Dutch Embassy and seemed quite lonely. After a couple years of fellowship with her, I had the joy of leading her to Christ. Not long after, her family came to visit and she left the city. Although I have not heard from her since, I still pray for her.

Christmas in Austria:

Our first Christmas away from our family was difficult. On that Christmas Sunday, we spoke to our son Tim and daughter-in-law Suzanne in California, listening as they described the blue velvet dress with a lace collar that Suzanne had just made for Nicole, our first grandchild. She would be participating in her first Christmas Church program that day. I so wanted to be there.

Later we went to our afternoon English International Chapel service. During the children's program a little girl came down the aisle wearing a blue velvet dress with a big white lace collar.

She walked in front of me and stood there, with the other children, as they were preparing to sing. My heart gasped and I began to fight tears. As I looked at her, I saw that I was frightening her. So, I thought…"This is a missionary kid and you are scaring her. These little ones need to know that a grandmother is a nice person, so stop feeling sorry for yourself and love these kids."

I also prayed that others back home would be a grandmother to my grandchildren!

While we lived in Vienna, we had many opportunities to love families, encourage moms in that culture and hang out with some teens. Some are still in touch with us today. The Lord taught us that He could indeed use a Grandma!!

Becoming a Guesthouse:

Our landlord often came to the lower level in our building to work as an architect. He offered us the use of an unused corner and helped us rent a space in the lower garage. When he decided to close down his office he offered to rent it to us to use as a guest room and a study. We presented this opportunity to our support group back in California and they immediately responded with the needed funds and we began another part of our ministry.

We bought some furniture in IKEA's second hand shop and began hosting other mission leaders; especially those who needed a short stay, relatives of staff, leaders from Eastern European countries who could get to Vienna, and even some family members.

Having an office and a guest apartment in the same space had its challenges. But most guests were out and about each day. We did not often need to feed the guests, but we did invite them up to our apartment in the early evening for an hour or so. We answered many questions and assisted them as we could.

Getting a driver's license in Austria

After being in Austria for only 10 months, we needed to apply for an Austrian driver's license. What a huge hurdle this can be, requiring weeks of studying manuals with the help of a translator.

The three part oral exam must be completed before the end of the first year of residence in Austria. We also had to present proof of successful completion of the Austrian First Aid course.

Phil writes: "Soon we will know the difference between a leitlinine, sperrlinie, haltlinie, odungslinine, richtungspfeile, and an aschriftzeichen, and perhaps a whole lot more!

Folks couldn't believe it when this old couple passed the exam on the first try! It was thanks to all the prayers and the neighbors who answered questions and tested us day after day.

Marriage Classes

During this whole time, we continued to travel and teach in various countries. There is no shortage of ministry opportunities here in Vienna and in this part of the world.

Soon after our first year in Vienna ended, Hans Finzel took a leave of absence and gave his duties of Human Resources director over to Phil, while I managed the in house weekly newspaper and the messages to be sent to various missions.

Phil continued teaching and traveling. I went along on most of the trips to help provide the cover story; that we were a couple out sightseeing. A married couple would not be viewed as suspiciously as two men might be.

As I sat in the back of many classrooms, I recorded the answers and the responses from the students. I also saw evidence of cheating on the exams! When the Marriage course was produced and Phil began teaching, I took part in some of the sessions. When the men brought their wives to the graduation, they asked for the same course for themselves.

In some cases, I taught while traveling with Phil. Other times, for security and convenience for the women, I traveled alone.

A Numerical Look at Our First Year in Austria

Ministry Trips:

> 1 trip to Romania

2 trips to Hungary

4 trips to Poland

Counseling:

Phil - 15 sessions with personnel/administration

Cindy - 28 sessions with singles and staff wives

Preaching opportunities;

Twice at International chapel

Twice at the Vienna Chinese Church

5 messages at an area SGA retreat

Administration:

25 staff conferences

2 new staff persons processed

14 prospective staff persons to communicate with...

117 letters written pertaining to personnel

Editing and publishing the weekly NEWSBRIEF and the bi-monthly   BEE INFORMED

Planned and executed the annual BEE retreat

Hospitality

126 Total guests in home

356 meals served to guests

7 Trips to airport to meet guests

2 Trips to train stations

Miscellaneous

Five weeks of German language study

Studying Romans/Galatians course

Studying Evangelism/Discipleship course

One week vacation

Study for Austrian Driver's license

Hundreds of letters and cards written to our supporters.

CHAPTER TEN

A View through Letters

Ecclesiastes 4:9-10: "Two are better than one; because they have a good return for their work; if one falls down, his friend can help him up. But pity the man who falls and has no one to help him up."

We had many wonderful adventures with Vienna as our home. We met so many faithful followers of Jesus. This chapter contains a variety of letters we sent to supporters during our time there.

Letter to Supporters and Family: December 1985

Dear Christian friends,

As I write this letter to you I have before me a photo of Margaret, a 9 year old girl we met in Eastern Europe this past summer. As we were carrying our luggage to the tiny cabin where we would be staying at the summer camp, there was Margaret.

She was seated on the dirt, drawing with a piece of coal onto a slab of weathered plywood. Despite the lack of paper, pen or paint, we could see immediately that she was a gifted artist. She happily showed us her drawings and we communicated as best we could, that she was most creative.

Over the next few days we noticed Margaret drawing on every piece of scrap material that she could find! When Cindy and I gave her a box of crayons which a friend back home had given us to bring to camp, you would have thought we had given Margaret a million dollars. She was so excited, and encouraged that she ran off to show her parents.

Margaret's parents were touched by our little gift to her. Her father is a brand new believer, who sat on the front row during meetings, listening carefully and attentively and taking notes. It encouraged my heart to see God at work in this little family. Margaret's mother was not a believer yet, but she became much more attentive.

This past week, we received a letter from behind the Iron Curtain! There was no name or return address or any printed message, only a child's drawing. It was of a blue cloud, with a red sun underneath the cloud. The bottom of the page is covered with a row of tiny flowers. The only writing is the word LOVE spelled out in big letters!

Included in the envelope were three tiny pictures of this precious family! It brought us both to tears. How exciting it is to see God's love at work-.encouraging families like this.

Thank you for being encouragers alongside us. May God bless you and your family as you love and encourage them this Christmas season.

Love,

Phil and Cindy

Letter written from Rossendaal, Holland: October 1985

Dear Friends,

In our last letter, Cindy asked if you would share with us what our reporting to you about the Church in Eastern Europe means to you. Thank you! It was great to read your responses.

Our primary mission this summer was to minister at family camps, a new outreach here in these parts. We worked primarily with a pastor we will call John who shared with us the pressures he is experiencing from denominational leaders, some of whom were compromising with the Communist leaders. Pastor John was under pressure for allowing teachers from the West to have influence.

A courageous man with a real burden for the lost souls of his country, John has refused to bow to the unbiblical ecclesiastical pressures. With his church behind him, they have separated completely from the denominational bondage.

Therefore they needed to find their own campgrounds for the summer ministry and chose a farm near a rural village. Although conditions were primitive, there was a tremendous spirit of unity and love. Meals were cooked in the house and carried out to be served in the barn! Afterwards, the barn was cleared to make room for the teaching sessions.

Teaching sessions were in the mornings with both men and women learning about the assurance of salvation, the character of God, the Godly marriage, and the Life of Elijah.

Cindy had afternoon sessions with the women, while the men watched the little ones and the older children played games or fished or went swimming. The women enjoyed crafts together and were excited with the gifts we were able to bring: sewing needles are difficult to find here and we were able to give each woman a supply of thread and needles.

The eldest camper was a 71 year old woman who accepted Christ last year. She had been a doctor in Russia many years ago and was baptized this year along with 17 other new Christians.

We met with several pastors to encourage them and determine how EEBM might help them, and had the opportunity to visit several house churches, one of which was a10 hour drive from our camp. The Christians there had quietly built a facility to hold 50 people, but the midweek service we attended had more than 80 people! They came on tractors and horse drawn carts for their first opportunity to attend a non-Catholic service and meet believers from the West!

All churches in Poland have long lines of people waiting to attend, as no one is kept from attending. There is only one rule: no teaching of children!

Soon we will be back traveling across the USA to share with you and thank you for your prayers. God has protected us as we traveled sometimes through heavy rains and floods!

As you pray for us, pray also for the pastors here, to have a heart for the souls of the people-they badly need more training and Bibles and materials.

Pray also for the new "underground seminary" being formed in Vienna: we are excited that our mission, EEBM, is a part of its formation. Pray for trained leaders to come to teach the men and women of Eastern Europe. The time has never been more ripe!

Blessings and our love,

Phil and Cindy

From a Letter to supporters: Dec. - Jan. 1989

Dear Faithful Supporters,

The other evening we sat in the dining room with our dear pastor friend from Poland, Pastor Joseph, and his wife Mary. (Honest those are their real names!) Their daughter and son-in-law and baby son were visiting with us over a delicious meal of soup, potatoes, meat and beets!

Pastor Joseph has a full time job with the coal mine, and travels frequently to Albania where he is constantly guarded. This pastor friend was delighted to receive a few special books from Phil to help him in sermon preparation and counseling.

Phil agreed to return to Poland in the spring to help Joseph begin a ministry with the men in his church, which thrilled Pastor Joseph!

After the meal, in another room, I had a chance to visit with the young couple. They have a new ministry singing and speaking in prison, and are excited about the many opportunities that are being presented to them. Many young people in Poland are in prison for petty theft and public drunkenness.

They shared with me some of the pressure of living with parents, with little hope of having an apartment of their own. Each of Mary and Joseph's older children lived with them for several years after they were married. I am certain Mary and Joseph are also weary of all these years of family responsibility, though they do not show it!

This young couple asked us to return to teach them how to form and lead small groups of young couples for fellowship, Bible study and encouragement.

Many young couples from Poland, East Germany and Hungary

are fleeing their homeland for a taste of material goods in the West. They are not considered to be political prisoners in their own country anymore. The western look in clothes, makeup, cars, and appliances is highly sought after.

Yet the shelves in the stores in Poland are bare! The shopkeepers stand around bored for there is nothing to sell. Everyone takes whatever they can to the borders where they must wait for hours to cross. Once in the West they sell whatever they have for goods and then go back through the arduous border crossing with their precious Western cargo, to use or to trade for food!

The prices for gasoline, meat, bread and milk are just the same as they are in Austria now, yet wages have not changed. The people are truly in great need.

We asked Pastor Joseph if it was a difficult time to be a pastor in Poland today. We know that this dear man has had a lifetime of difficulty, living through war, years of communism, and persecution because of his protestant faith in a strong Catholic nation. "Were these days difficult too, we asked?"

With a big smile Joseph told us that difficult experiences only make the Christian believer stronger. He felt privileged to be a pastor during these times, and wanted to be better equipped to reach out to the hungry and confused people of his country.

Walls are coming down, border guards are even smiling now, and confusion is everywhere. Russia continues to open up in exciting ways. Many teams are traveling there now. Other countries are re-establishing seminaries, and we are helping them. Specific needs for specific ministries are being requested; this is truly an exciting and demanding time to serve in this part of the world!

The walls are still tight around Albania, Bulgaria and Roma-

nia. We know that the Lord is at work inside and so we ask you to continue to be faithful in your prayers for God's power to move in the hearts of the God less leaders there. Isn't your faith a bit stronger, seeing Him work so mightily in these other once closed countries? Mine is!

Pray for Mary and Joseph

Pray for our promise for a continuing ministry with them

Pray that we will be faithful to what HE has called us to do…..

And from yet another letter:

Dear Friends,

We want to share with you Alina's story:

We had driven out of Austria, across Czech to Poland. Crossing a border was always an exciting adventure. There were questions to answer and papers to have stamped and of course the inspection of our car. After the crossing into Poland, we spent the night at a border hotel.

After a long day of travel, we were glad to have a place to rest.

However, we first needed to buy tickets and ask for instructions to various 'sightseeing' places in Southern Poland. Of course, we would not actually go there but we needed to appear to be retired Americans on a sightseeing tour.

After breakfast the next morning, we packed up for our first visit to a Polish doctor who had gathered about a dozen of his young men for Phil to teach as part of the underground seminary. Dr. Henryk was from a Lutheran background and had married a young architect, Alina, who shared his passion for sharing Christ. She was also from a strong believer's background. Her father, though employed by the Polish government to design coalmines, was secretly a pastor. He often travelled to Albania to work, and told us about the conditions in that very cold, and closed to the gospel country.

Henryk, Alina, and their two small children lived in a row house development in Ustron. We drove to their little town and parked below their house near the Catholic Church, backing up to a coal pile with lots of trees nearby to keep our car hidden. We walked to the back door and did as we were always instructed to do: we didn't knock, but opened the door and walked in as though we lived there!

No one was at home when we arrived so we sat quietly until Dr. Henryk arrived. After hugging us, he turned on some music and told us to whisper. He would be reported and possibly arrested if he had foreign guests in his home. Guests, other than family members had to be reported to the village mayor. And of course it was most illegal to have a church meeting without permission.

Henryk took Phil to meet with the other men in a mountain cabin not too far away. I was told to wait for Alina to come home, but not to turn on any lights or flush the toilet! When Alina arrived at home with her children, she was surprised to see me but very gracious. After fixing supper for us and putting the children to bed, we began to visit.

I asked her to share with me what her life was like and how she came to know Jesus as her Savior. Our long talk had to stop whenever the music stopped, and then begin again. She shared with me that often the police would come and search the house, taking away Bibles and any papers which spoke about Christ. They had developed hiding places, some out in the forest in caves!

She told me that sometimes when the police would come and take Henryk away, she would lay on the floor pleading with tears for God to bring him back. The children would cry and beg mommy to get up off the floor and not to cry. She told me how the neighbors would report anything suspicious to earn special favor with the government. In those days of rationing, the special favors would include the ability to purchase meat and sugar and other hard to find items.

I asked her to share her story and especially how she came to trust Jesus as her personal Savior with a friend or two, and that the next time we got together we would talk about it.

After midnight, Alina had gone to bed while I slept on the couch. When Dr. Henryk came back with Phil, I reported that I so enjoyed my visit with Alina.

Dr. Henryk then asked me to teach his wife: he wanted to share Christ with other men and their wives and to build a group of men and women who would reach Poland for Christ! The next time I came with Phil there were about seven women in the living room waiting for me. I was confused and worried about security, but Alina explained that it was all right, that they had made some good excuses for holding a meeting.

These women had been gathered as I had asked her to do. They had taught each other all they knew about the gospel and they were waiting for more teaching from me! I found that they were meeting at the bus stop in the mornings to pray and encourage one another and then they would go share the love of Christ with women that they knew. Often they would take bread or soup to share with others. It did not matter if the women were believers or not, just that they were in need!

We began a course of study called The Character of God. I shared with them that when tough times come into our lives, what we know to be true about God is what carries us through! After meeting with them for a year, I was surprised to learn that they had been discussing a plan to hold a conference for the women of the area.

There was the possibility of using the hall that the Catholics used for their widows. Catholic widows in Poland with no one to care for them were called Deacons, and lived in a communal hall, and were allowed to use their main dining hall for meetings.

I was asked to go speak to the Deacons. I went and asked them if they would encourage and pray for the young women. The younger women did not like the Deacons who they felt scolded them too much about things like their children wearing soiled clothes.

I then asked the young women to begin praying for the hearts of these old women and to smile and thank them for instructions. Later I asked the old women to each choose a young woman and begin praying for her and speaking kindly to her.

After a few months of this interaction, the young women asked to use the Hall for a daylong meeting to encourage other women. We chose the topic, "What a Godly Woman Looks Like." Alina brought together a team of women who played beautiful music, shared testimonies and I gave several talks. Tapes of the meeting were later distributed all over Poland.

The women brought their own bread and meat or cheese in their purses and ate when they were hungry. The meeting began at 9:00 a.m. and continued until dark when the last bus left the area.

Alina asked for a show of hands as to which villages they represented and and you could see the women connecting in fellowship. God was at work and it was so exciting! Women were given the opportunity to accept Christ and others were given places where they could meet to learn more about Jesus.

Alina continues today to minister all over Poland and in neighboring countries. She and Henryk counsel and train pastors and leaders, and conduct conferences. Recently Alina sent me a message that in the village's new hotel, over a thousand women attended their Women's Day celebration. Alina's daughter, Estera, was one of the principal speakers!

Presently, Alina and Henryk are teaming up with some young Catholic leaders in their country, aiming to reach Poles for Christ!

One individual committed to Christ, then his family, then his village and now his nation!

What does it take to do all this?

Patience is perseverance under pressure.

Henryk and Alina teach us that opposition develops the Godliest patience you can imagine....

CHAPTER ELEVEN

Join the Adventure

Jeremiah 29:11: "For I know the plans I have for you,' declares the Lord... "plans to prosper you and not to harm you, plans to give you hope and a future."

"WANT TO VISIT A CLASS WITH US?"

When we saw the line of cars parked alongside a tiny road and the people waiting outside the small building, we knew we were in the right place!_

We had hoped to find the meeting place in time for the Sunday morning service, but the long wait at the gas station delayed us. Now it was almost noon, and we had no idea what to expect. None of our mission teams had ever visited this group of believers before, but we had received an official invitation to begin a training course with them. We were on another adventure.

Come along!

As we parked our car and walked toward the house church a man came out to greet us and ushered us through the crowds into the church, right up to the platform. The final song was in process and the service was ending.

But plans were meant to be changed, as the service would indeed continue because there were special guests present! The men's choir sang another song and the interpreter came forward to welcome us and invite Phil to the platform.

Phil was careful not to speak too long. After all, the service had already been going for four hours! It was crowded, but the children were outdoors playing. In this Eastern bloc country, no children, not even teenagers are allowed to attend a gospel service.

Struggling with the Lord over the decision to study for the ministry, our translator confessed that the Lord had spoken to his heart during the service! He had just been told by his sweetheart that she would not marry him if he continued to pursue the ministry. He felt so encouraged that the Lord had sent us to minister to him in such a specific way.

Many crowded around us after the message, their smiles and hugs conveying the love and oneness which we all were feeling....despite the barriers of language, the Holy Spirit can bind us together in unity!

Another adventure was waiting: we were asked to ride to one of the believer's homes for dinner before the afternoon teaching sessions. Five big adults and one child climbed into our small car, meant for 4 medium adults...and off we went.

Soon we stopped at one of the high rise apartment buildings. They were so ugly: no markings on them, porches filled with clothes drying on a line, no flowers, no grass, no trees, just plain government housing. They all looked the same and I wondered how you could remember which one was yours.

Up the stairs we all climbed and I wondered where the elevator was. Later, when I saw how tiny and old it was, I realized that climbing up six flights wasn't so bad after all.

Seated at a long table made up of several tables pushed together, we were served delicious soup followed by plates piled with rice, meat patties and beets.

Over dinner we learned that our host's group was eager to study as nearly all of the men had churches to pastor, and none had any formal Biblical training. All had other jobs as the churches were not able to financially support them.

We barely finished the meal when the coffee was served and it wasn't even *settled* yet when it was announced that it was time to go. Coffee is a special treat in this country and is made with hot water poured over the grounds in your cup. You stir it a bit, and then let it sit to let the grounds settle. But there was no time today!

Arriving back at the meeting place we noticed that our group of students had grown quite a bit! They were excited to meet each other and to study in what they called a 'systematic way".

One man, an ambulance driver, had travelled for 6 hours on the train to attend class and later in the evening he would get back on the train to return to his job. There was an architect who asked us to pray for his plan to start many new churches throughout his county. Many buildings would need to be remodeled from private homes into church facilities.

There were engineers, a doctor, and several ironworkers among the students.

Much time was spent explaining the sacrifice of time necessary to complete the course, but the men seemed to welcome the challenge. One man said, *"if you will come all this way to help us, we must do our best and more."*

Our spirits soared as we drove to a hotel that night and made preparations for an early morning departure to the next new class. Another eight hour drive was ahead of us, but what a privilege it was to teach those who were so eager to learn and serve Christ!

The next evening the class was four times larger and just as eager to begin. One man said; "I have read the first lesson and already I had the opportunity to use the study to help someone else, I can see that this will be most useful for me." Another said that his wife was always taking his new book and studying it, and a third told us that his whole family was studying the material.

All were mature leaders and pastors of churches, but without formal theological or Bible training. Each one had to work at another job each day to support their families.

This is just the story of one trip: Each visit is just as full of new faces, new testimonies, new challenges and the opportunity to remind the believers that they are not alone. Each trip we take gives us the chance to tell our brothers and sisters that the body of Christ in America knows and cares about them.

Listen to Phil as he shares what happed in Poland in 1989:

Praise the Lord for a great trip to Poland and Czechoslovakia. We had good border crossings, and despite a bit of sleet and rain, we also had good weather. What a thrill it was to see over 400 men from different denominations and house churches gather in Warsaw and dedicate themselves afresh to the Lord, all with one purpose: to reach Poland for Christ.

Luis Palau was our speaker teaching on personal holiness, family life and prayer for your city and Poland. We were even led in prayer for government leaders.

It was both a joy and privilege to feel the unity of these men in these special days. Please pray for us as we have been asked to travel to the Soviet Union in the spring to teach. It will be a rigorous and demanding trip where we will be sleeping on the train and teaching every day. And as always, we will be learning about the problems and stresses of the daily lives of the believers.

Pray for me as I deal with currency values, cultural differences, customs and transportation. We will be observing the tightest security measures and must be "wise as serpents and harmless as doves. We need your prayers!

And this is what I wrote about our trip to the Soviet Union in 1989:

Thanks for praying for us during our teaching trip to the Soviet Union. We thought you might enjoy hearing about our travels and teaching times in Tallin, Riga, Kiev and Moscow!

We were surprised to find that at customs they were only checking for diamonds and precious stones and didn't spend too much time with us. We weren't even asked if we had books or Bibles or cassette players, which was fortunate, as we had a number of these! We were so glad to be able to safely bring in all our material for the classes – The Lord had it all arranged that the subject of the day would be precious stones!

We were met by a black car and taken to the hotel. We soon learned to respect the "black cars," which took us to airports and trains and were on a tight previously arranged itinerary.

While in the cities we did not have an arranged tour and we used public transportation to get to the classes. I am grateful that Phil was able to read the signs! The metro was fast and direct, but sometimes finding the right street after we got off was a challenge!

We would receive directions such as, 'walk until you see the tipped over house and then turn right." The problem was that often there was more than one tipped over house! At times we would hear the people singing, and follow the music to the class. Over and over we were warned that despite the changes and increases in freedoms, the KGB was still very active and still gathering information.

Such a contrast we saw in these classes: one was like a group of young mavericks, eager to challenge everything. Another group was gentle and sincere, having spent much time in prison. One of these men showed us a tiny spoon he had created out of bread while he was in prison. He made sculptures out of bread to bring home as gifts to his wife.

In yet another class, all the students came well dressed in suits and ties and demonstrated their appreciation for us by asking, "What can we do to help you during your visit?" Phil asked them to pray for the classes and the personal study time for each student, asking them to hold one another accountable to share what they have learned with others.

One man travelled for four days to ask us to come to his city next. Of course Phil spent time with him to learn the details!

Teaching from Galatians and Romans Phil explained that the reason for the course is to make certain that our lives and actions are based on the Word of God, not personal convictions or Church tradition. Phil pleads with them to compare every belief against the Word of God and communicate God's word to others with love, not judgment.

But a man interrupts, "what about the brother who is weak in the faith and lets the hair on his head and face grow?" Another man speaks out, "What about the woman who has gold in her ears and claims to be a believer?"

Yes - discussion time is very lively here – but the worship is so moving! Time is spent in beautiful singing and prayer, some weeping, others with hands lifted, others on their knees. The men are in true fellowship with our Lord and prayer time only ends when the leader begins to pray out loud.

I was able to slip away from the class in Moscow to attend a worship service in the Baptist Church there. The wife of the pastor, Vera, led me to a section of the church roped off and filled with tourists.

Suddenly the majority of the tourists got a signal and they stood up to go, leaving me alone until a long line of others waiting for a seat came and sat down. No eye contact was made with anyone during the service until it was time for communion. Those who wished to take communion stood and an elder came and looked into their eyes as you tore the bread and drank from the same glass cup as all the others had. I could see several policemen on the lower level who stepped forward to observe those who stood for communion…

Later, an altar call was given and one man ran to the front, shouting and crying as he confessed his sins before the whole congregation- and the police! An amazing experience indeed!

Another moving experience during our Moscow trip took place on a cold winter afternoon when Vera took me to a prayer group of women. No lights were on in the unheated room where a precious group of ladies had gathered to privately pray for things on their hearts and for their nation. There was no leader or program – they just prayed!

Vera asked if I wanted to talk with one of the women and she touched one dear old lady on the shoulder and asked her what she was praying about. She answered that she was asking God to touch her nation.

I was touched to see that these dear women were the poorest of the poor. Their shoes were not the warm boots that were needed for the weather, but were home made of felt and fur. Despite their own personal needs, these ladies were on their knees in prayer for their nation.

Years later, in Korea, I witnessed a similar group while we were there teaching a class. Our guest room was on the top floor of the church and I could hear singing in the early hours of the morning. One morning I crept out to find that it was a prayer service. A woman brought a pair of shoes to the stage and placed them near the pulpit – now what was that all about, I wondered?

She was the greatest 'soul winner" of the church, the pastor explained, and she would ask for a piece of clothing from those she met. She especially liked to bring a pair of someone's shoes and place them near the pulpit and ask God to fill that person with His Spirit, so that one day they could stand in church and give God glory for saving them.

I have been blessed and amazed to see God at work in the lives of women all around the world: first in their own lives, and then in the lives of others. First one home, then a family, then a village, and then a nation!

Did you enjoy your trip with us this time?

CHAPTER TWELVE

1991

Ephesians 3:14-17: "For this reason I kneel before the Father from whom his whole family in heaven and on earth derives its name. I pray that out of his glorious riches, he may strengthen you with power through his Spirit in your inner being."

Phil and I were thrilled to travel to Estonia in 1991. So many changes were happening throughout Eastern Europe. Listen to how Phil describes our trip:

We were able to fly via the Air Force out of Delaware: a C-141 made for rather rough accommodations but for $10.00 we kept smiling! After resting for two nights in Germany, we rented a car, drove to Vienna, repacked and made travel arrangements: we travelled to Budapest by train then by plane to Estonia for some seminars. Then off to Moscow.

Yes, the travel was exhausting, but we have seen some wonderful changes.

From a support letter in February 1991.

Estonia and more!

Because we had an official invitation to Estonia, we could make our own arrangements and stay in private homes. What a thrill to feel the vibrant national spirit in this country which declared its independence only three months ago! There is much confusion and many shortages but these small nations of the Baltic are filled with enthusiasm.

Tallin, Estonia is a beautiful seaport: the narrow, winding streets remind me of Western Europe. The climate and diet of the people is much like Helsinki, Finland, which is, of course, just a few miles away.

As we walked to the BEE seminar held in the city, our translator told us of the difficulties and problems that many of the citizens had faced in recent years. The church where our next class would be held was a Catholic cathedral, which had been taken away from the Catholics and all the church denominations were forced to meet together in this same building! The Communist government thought that this would cause division among Christians. However, just the opposite happened!

At the end of the street, across from the church, we could see a huge building which used to house the KGB- it was dark and empty with the building sealed. Yet across the street, the lights were on in the church! The church was alive and the KGB was closed!

What a striking illustration that God is truly in control, as He always has been, even though at times these dear people, must have felt that that they were forgotten. I am still learning that I can trust Him to fulfill His purposes in my life, my children's lives, and in the lives of the people to whom we have been sent to encourage and teach.

We rode the train all night to Riga, Latvia and were met by a colleague, who took us to our hotel. Arrangements had been made by a local pastor and we were able to pay for our five day stay in the local currency - it came to $7.00!

There was a shortage of food which affected us, but the greatest challenge was finding taxis, airplanes and private cars for our travels. We did lots of walking and praying for transportation to the next class or the next city.

There was one class in Riga where we could not locate our contact by telephone, and fearing that the class had been rescheduled we took a long taxi ride to his church. There is always a bit of anxiety when you dismiss your only means of transportation, and you find yourself in the middle of now where! Having no idea what would happen next we were encouraged to see a light on at the church!

Inside, we met some young women who did not speak any English or German, but very politely asked us to sit "one moment." After a short wait, the young leader came to explain that he had just that day returned from Siberia where he and a group of Russian believers were conducting a ministry from a boat to villages in the countryside. He was excited to report that scores of people were coming to Christ. His class members were out doing ministry!

Some of his seminar students were staying behind to follow up, and he was planning to leave that night to return to them with supplies. What a thrill to hear reports of this ministry bearing fruit and to see the joy in this leader's heart.

One of the requirements BEE has for its students is that each course must be shared with others for a student to continue to study with us! I often ask myself, "What if the church in America was to enforce such a rule? What if American believers could not attend another Bible class or listen to another sermon until they shared it with five others?"

Next we traveled to Minsk, Byelorussia, where we stayed in a private home. The food shared with us was tasty and abundant - lots of potatoes. Yet our host told us that the crops had done poorly the previous two years and his family would find it difficult in the coming winter! But with a big smile on his face, he said... "But that is not my concern -it is my Heavenly Father's job to feed my family. My job is to share the Gospel!"

Before his conversion to Christ, this leader was a highly respected scientist. He had helped start a new church and with the BEE training, he could become the pastor. Also directing a ministry for the needy in Minsk, this prospective pastor led an outreach ministry to a remote part of Russia as well.

While Phil taught the class of pastors and leaders, I was taken to a gathering of about one hundred women: It was the first meeting they had ever had with a woman speaker! And she was from the West...she was me!

Crowded together into a newly remodeled and freshly painted room, older women in head scarves sat on long benches in front of me. To my right the younger married women sat, nearly all of them pregnant. To my left were the unmarried women hoping to hear my lecture, but as the pastor in charge told me…"They can be excused if you wish to speak at any time with only married women'!

I assured the pastor in charge that what I had to say would be appropriate for everyone to hear and in particular for the young women.

We had a great time discussing the women of the Bible and how God used them. We talked about how they, as women, could impact their families and their nation for God.

Later, the pastor wanted to ask me some questions because he needed to know how he could help these women. So with the women listening intently, we asked them what kind of help they needed. They wanted to know how to teach their children about Christ - with no materials. We decided that there were gifted women in that group who could write stories and others would draw a simple cartoon of the characters in the story.

Other women wanted to know how to share the salvation message and what verses to use. I suggested that each one write out her story to share during future meetings. The answers for the pastor were all right there in that group.

As usual, I spent some time playing with the children, letting them teach me some new words and giving them a sentence or two to recite. Staying in their homes is a great way to build relationships and minister to them. One pastor when saying goodbye to us pointed to his new bathtub (not yet hooked up) and said. "Next time you may go for a swim!"

Our lives have been so blessed and we've met so many courageous and thoughtful brothers and sisters. Later, Phil and I traveled to Romania for God's next big adventure in our lives. It was on this trip that we met Pastor Josef.

Romania: November 1991

On a Sunday afternoon, after attending a four hour church service where 20 adults were baptized, we had lunch with Pastor Josef and a dozen other guests. When we asked Josef to share with us some of his stories of the difficult times he shared this....

"I was brought in for questioning by the Securitate often...the most notable occasion being the day before the Revolution broke out."

He was ordered to appear at the police station at 8:00 A.M, and taken to the basement and questioned, "Why do you continue to teach children and young people about Jesus? "and "Why do you meet with these people from the West?"

He was asked about his travels to Moldavia and Russia, where he took Bibles and participated in a ministry there. All was then illegal in Romania and Russia.

Answering the charges with his own personal testimony, he told them he had to answer to God. He said, "It was more frightening to me to disobey God than the Securitate!"

Growing angry, his interrogators left him for the rest of the day in a dark, cold cell. When they returned late in the afternoon, they asked if he had changed his mind.

 "Oh thank you for this quiet day," he answered, "I have been so busy: this is a special gift for me to be able to sit here all day, with no interruptions, to be able to fast and pray for my people. I have been praying that they would be strong in the Lord!

Of course his answer made the police all the angrier!

The day before the Revolution broke out, he was called in again and told to go home and prepare his family: the next morning he was to report for a three year prison sentence. That evening at home, Josef said he slept like a baby, knowing that the Lord would take care of him and his family.

The police phoned in the morning to tell him that they had more important business in the capital: Josef's prison sentence never came about because the Revolution changed everything.

Josef told us, "I just thought….well, praise the Lord in prison or preaching, whatever the Lord wants ….I am ready!"

There were, of course, many other difficult situations for Josef.

He and Maria and their three children had lived for fifteen years in three tiny rooms above the church in very primitive conditions. After the Revolution, a neighbor came to ask for forgiveness. He confessed having allowed a closet in his house to be used by the Securitate to listen to Josef's family conversations and church meetings.

For many years the Securitate had a car parked in front of their home. Their home would be watched day and night. Often Josef would go out to invite the men to come inside, asking them if they wanted some warm tea. Sometimes the police would smile, but usually they turned away as he spoke.

Josef told us, "You cannot be imprisoned by another person's fear….give love in the presence of fear!"

As Josef was speaking to us, I watched the face of a fifteen year old American boy, who was a part of a mission team visiting from the U.S. He was deeply moved by Josef's testimony, and I knew that Josef had left a mark on this young man's heart forever.

Our church back home had a heart for Romania. They had given us some money to give to Josef and Maria, who delightedly told us they would use it to purchase their first washing machine! We rejoiced with them to hear that another ministry from the West had just purchased a home for them.

Romanians are a responsive people, with a great love of music and poetry. A music festival was held while we visited: I saw 30 mandolins, 6 violins, 1 flute, 1 base viola and some very large mandolins being played by all ages. They played "Onward Christian Soldiers" in our honor and it was like being welcomed into a large and loving Christian family.

Josef had plans to develop an orphanage, a book store, an outreach to the poor, a clinic for basic health care, a Bible school, and a BEE training center! He was given some land and a few buildings after the Revolution, as a part of the reparations being made to some who had been deeply tormented by the government.

At first, some wanted Josef to run for a government position, but he asked instead for buildings and property in the center of the city.

Sunday dinner was nearly over now and we were still deeply engulfed in Josef's story when someone arrived and interrupted Josef….

Josef turned, announcing that we must leave now: there were severe economic troubles in the Capital and transportation might soon be shut down. We needed to leave right away to catch the last train so that we might reach our flight back to Vienna the next day.

Without time to prepare ourselves or say proper goodbyes we were ushered to the pastor's taxi. His son ran in and secured us tickets and seats on the train. The train was so crowded that it was difficult to move through the aisles.

Sitting down, I peeked at the package the pastor's wife had thrust into my hands at the last minute: it was two dark purple cut-glass glasses. Our generous friends always gave a gift of something…..

A Romanian train ride is quite the adventure!

The farmer's wife who sat acres the row from me, had a huge sack above her head, it was filled with cabbage, and at her feet was a plastic bucket filled with fuel oil. As she stared at me I couldn't help but wonder what she was thinking. We were the ones who had invaded her world. We were the strange ones in the train that afternoon!

It was already dark when we reached the capitol. After dealing with a surly taxi driver, we stopped at a hotel where the clerk told us there were no available rooms. Knowing that God would provide for us, we told him we would be happy to wait, as surely someone would fail to show. We only had to wait on a sofa for a half an hour when a room opened up. Thank you Lord!

What a delight to enjoy a clean, warm room and hot showers after the train ride. We were weary and needed a good rest. From our hotel window we could see Ceaucescu's Palace and all the buildings which had played such a prominent part during the Revolution.

Monday was indeed a banker's nightmare: the exchange rate went wild. After some struggle to use our Austrian currency, we were able to get a few dollars to buy breakfast. We were lucky to get a safe taxi ride to the airport and later learned that there were several riots in Bucharest in the following days.

We learned from Josef and Maria that things now cost five times more than just two months previous. Winter will be a challenge for them and it will be difficult to build the church.

Yet, in the land where churches were once bulldozed, there rises a new church giving glory to God. In the land where smuggled Bibles were turned into toilet paper, hundreds now turn to Christ. In the land where believers were beaten, imprisoned, and died, now rises a church purified and on fire for Christ.

People want to come here by the dozens, pastors, doctors, and the young: It is not so much what they can do for Romania, as it is that those from the West want to be exposed to these courageous, spirit-filled people.

O Father, I pray…..

For faith to believe that You rule the world in truth and righteousness.

For faith to take no anxious thought for tomorrow, but to believe in the continuance of your past mercies;

For faith to put my own trust in love rather than in force, when other men harden their hearts against me…

For faith to profit by such sufferings as You call upon me to endure.

For faith as seen in Josef and Maria and those other godly examples who have gone before….

CHAPTER 13

A Time of Transition

Revelation 21:5: "He who was seated on the throne said, "Behold, I am making all things new."

Changes in Eastern Europe

Many changes were slowly taking place in Eastern Europe. Due to uprisings and strikes and demonstrations, we saw many people in the summer of 1989 fleeing out of their countries on the trains, seeking safe places in Europe.

Dramatic photos and TV programs showed us the Berlin Wall being taken down: some of our staff left immediately to witness the event and brought back pieces of the wall.

The countries had to decide how to handle their freedom and the church and its leadership had to pray and discern how to use the openness that was rather suddenly given to them.

Sometimes we would travel a great distance to meet with people only to find that they had taken off to minister in some needy place. We encouraged them, prayed with them and gave them more materials if they wanted them.

In other places the pastors got visions of much larger facilities, and grew bold, asking for the best spots in the city or the best materials and often the new governments gave what they had requested. It was truly a beautiful time to see God at work blessing His faithful ones.

Moving to Moscow to Help Begin a Church: 1991

At this time we got a rather unusual request: to go back to Moscow and work with a newly formed church which John Maisel had begun. We were asked to be there only for a few months until they could equip an American pastor to come and serve permanently.

This group of about 400 souls had never been in church before. These new believers were former KGB and military and Soviet teachers and were not yet trusted and welcomed by other churches, so we helped them form a church.

Working with folks from various backgrounds was not at all common here, and working with folks who needed to grow deep in their personal faith, trust God, overlook personal annoyances of others, and to love others was a challenge!

But our supporters prayed and God provided all that we needed, even a gifted children's worker from the USA who came and gave her life for families. Up until this point, children had not been allowed in churches.

I well remember a great Christmas Celebration that went on almost one whole day: there were pageants, singing, testimonies, messages, and more singing. The people did not want to stop! .

We had given out Bibles to the faithful after the Billy Graham crusade left a store house of Bibles for us to share.

Every day, except Saturday morning, was given to a teaching group in our home and in the little office that Phil was able to procure down town. At times there were demonstrations so wild we had to fight our way through to walk home. Exciting days for certain!

One sweet memory I have of those days, was when Phil brought home a small freshly baked loaf of bread! He was walking home because the tram was too crowded, when he smelled fresh bread. He followed the smell along with others on the street and came upon a basement window through which folks were selling bread. Bread was not easy to find in those days and he and I enjoyed that treat!

Memories of Moscow I will never forget:

Old ladies selling their personal belongings on the street; too proud to beg, but so needy, unable to afford bread or potatoes…

Seeing children begging on the street, not in school because the teachers were on strike or searching for food.

Our proud scientist friend, embarrassed that we should see his city of Moscow so poor.

Long lines of people waiting for a McDonald's hamburger, or bread, or gasoline, or underwear.

Believers asking for more time with you as they asked for explanations for Bible passages…how they need study materials!

Believers content with a cup of tea, and no food when they come to study, even when you know they have not eaten.

A string quartet playing music before the church service who only knew one hymn: Ave Maria!

Watching God turn hearts toward Him, in His love...

Walking through Red Square with a sense of peace everywhere.... finally!

The black cars which used to inspire fear, no longer being a cause for concern anymore...

Lenin's tomb with a short line of mostly Westerners...

CHAPTER FOURTEEN

Back to the U.S.S.R.!

*Matthew. 11:28: "Come to me and I will give you rest…all who work
so hard and carry a heavy yoke. Wear my yoke for it will fit perfectly
and let me teach you.…For I am gentle and humble. And you will
find rest for your souls; for I give you only light burdens"*

We left for the airport on a beautiful morning for our fourth missionary trip of the year to the Soviet Union! We were to meet with several classes in the Moscow area, then fly to assist a class in Siberia that had been trying to get started, and then on to Leningrad.

I was told that in each place, "the women are expecting you." My heart's desire was to encourage the wives of the male students. They worked long hours, faced a continual struggle to find food, and shouldered most of the burden of caring for their homes and children.

The men all had outside jobs in addition to pastoring at least one church and sometimes several! One man told me that his wife was not able to attend services as she had no proper shoes!

Below is my account of what two weeks in Russia looked like from May 15-26. Each day brought new insight in God's magnificence and the deep need in the U.S.S.R. for the gospel.

May 15

Do you have more than $15?

After a good flight to Moscow we found ourselves stuck in a slow baggage claim, due to a newly posted rule: "*If you have more than $15 you need to go through the red line.*" Who would possibly be traveling with less than $15? We asked a few questions and a new line was opened up. As we passed through, no one bothered to even inspect our luggage! Ah Russia…

We were surprised to find new wallpaper and wood closets at our familiar hotel. However, the same old toilet remained, with the cheapest toilet seat I have ever seen -it is stored *behind* the toilet *and you are to pull it out when you might want to use it*!

We had a nice dinner in a smoke filled restaurant in the hotel. Unless you were registered at a hotel, it was impossible to buy a meal in Moscow without waiting in line for hours. We didn't know it at the time, but that was to be the best meal of our trip: beef roulade, potatoes, cucumbers, Pepsi, and brown bread

Leaving the hotel, we found a phone booth and called our first contact. Yes, they were expecting us the next evening and yes we knew how to take public transportation.

May 16: First Class

Breakfast was an odd assortment: bread, butter, beet salad, fish salad, and hot farina, spoiled yogurt to put on top, apple jam, and mystery meat balls. I ate a simple meal: farina, tea and bread.

Leaving the hotel we found a phone, confirmed our assignments and then walked to the Pushkin Art Gallery, then later to the main Intourist hotel. It only cost us $1.50 for a buffet lunch: gristly beef in tomato sauce, cold french fries, cucumber, bread and tea. This was our main meal for the day.

More phone calls to have our directions confirmed were made using various phones - So much time was spent confirming the logistics of travel!

Finally we headed off to our first class as the evening grew cold and rainy. The leader had once been an artist and was now working as a pastor. We were fortunate that his wife was an excellent translator.

They had been studying the Evangelism/Discipleship course, and we were excited to hear one student say, "Before this class, I did not think that I would be qualified to share Christ, now I see it is as God's will and His plan for me....I must do it!"

The Lord had already used him to share with one lady and the others who overheard their conversation formed a small group to study with him! He was so happy to be able to clearly present the Gospel.

That night we were treated to a car ride back to our hotel. The class leader and his friend own and operate a car together. Paul was given the car by Christians in East Germany and his friend bought the license: so together they are able to operate a car!

May 18: Veterans at the Kremlin

After our morning study time, being the nice tourists that we were, we visited the Armory of Moscow and walked through the Kremlin looking up at the Russian Orthodox Cathedrals. They were not churches any more but museums.

It was the time of year when veterans from the last two wars gathered in Moscow for reunions and to be honored. We took some pictures of some of the older men with rows of military ribbons pinned on their chests: they seemed so pleased by the attention!

This day's class went very well: we were thrilled to see growth in the unity and spirit of the class. The previous year we had been concerned about this group: they were like mavericks. Now we saw a sense of love and encouragement amongst them: they had learned to apply their studies to their lives!

May 19: Mending a Marriage

I will never forget this day! The night before one of the students asked if I would have time to talk to his wife as she had not come to the meeting for women. In the morning he surprised us by showing up across the street from our hotel. He had been waiting for us to come out and he told Phil he wanted me to go with him immediately! How very Russian that he asked Phil - not me!!

He was having difficulty in his marriage and he took me by subway, tram, bus and then by foot for an hour and a half to his home in north Moscow to meet his wife, Luba.

Luba was a beautiful dark-haired young woman, with two lively little boys. As we entered the home, I could see three American men seated in the living room. I greeted them but they remained a bit secretive! I can guess what mission they might represent!

As a dentist, Luba was busy. Besides her job, and caring for her sons and home, she often had to entertain her husband's guests from the Evangelistic Center. When we sat in the kitchen to talk, I found that Luba had thrown all of her husband's study books out the window into the snow bank. She had made quite a statement and I had been brought in to settle this family squabble!

I decided it was a good idea to ask Peter to leave us alone for awhile!

Looking around I noticed how beautiful the kitchen was: in typical Russian style the cupboards were brightly colored, with flowers painted on them. I remarked how beautiful and creative it was and Luba told me that her husband had done it, as well as making their bed, table, chairs and the boys' furniture.

After a tour of her home we spent three hours together sharing our testimonies, encouraging one another and studying what the Bible has to say about God's design for the role of the woman.

Peter came back and made tea for us as we all talked about how to strengthen their marriage. They were eager to make it work - there were just too many busy things in the way. How often I have heard this and have felt it in my own marriage through the years! Ministry and marriage… can they coexist?

Just as we were beginning to really talk, Peter's aunt and mother came in the door for a visit. I watched as they brought in a live chicken, killed it on the window sill, cleaned it in hot water, fried it and served up a meal of chicken, rice, cucumbers and tea!

The ladies had come from Uzbek, their heads covered with scarves, with weathered faces and hands. One had no teeth and found it difficult to chew so food was cut for her. They brought candy for the boys and Luba was not very happy about that. I guess it is universal that Grandmothers do these things!

With nine of us around the table, we finished our meal and stood for a prayer afterwards, as is the custom in a believer's home. Things soon settled down and the boys played in another room and we sat back at the clean table with tea to discuss what we had learned that day.

Pulling back one chair, I said that Jesus was sitting there with us, and asked Luba and Peter to each write down what they would like Jesus to do in their partner's life. Lists were written and they were to exchange them and pray over the requests each day. In one week they were to meet again and see what God had done in their lives!

They were very quiet but content as we prayed together. Peter accompanied me back on the same long journey to the hotel, where Phil was waiting for me with tickets to the circus. It was a nice and needed break: what a day!

Later on I asked a couple to meet with Peter and Luba: they took them to a marriage conference in another country. Peter and Luba have since used the story of their marriage to minister to many other couples.

May 20: Off to Siberia!

After a day of sightseeing, we arrived at the airport, ready to leave Moscow for Novosibersk, Siberia. The airport was filthy and smoky and our flight was delayed. We finally took off at 3 a.m. and arrived, very tired, at noon only to find that our accommodations were not what we had ordered!

Due to our late arrival, our first class spot was given away. First class in Russia meant a private bath, some food and a clean bed! We found that we had no hot water and only soup, ice cream and some kind of smelly fish. The management kindly promised a refund, but we had to stay put!

We enjoyed meeting new people, many of German heritage, and many from the Technical University, like Lydia:

Lydia was a 'flotation surveyor/architect' employed by the government who spoke fluent German but wanted to study in English. Together we went over her testimony in English, and worked on correctly pronouncing the books of the Bible. A very bright pastor's daughter, her goal was to be an English Bible translator.

The people here seemed very different from others we had met in the USSR. They were survivors, having been here for two or three generations of exile. Those in exile had been leaders or poets or professionals ousted from Moscow.

We spent two days getting the classes off to a good start. Some of the older men were progressing very quickly and a new plan was made for them to teach the younger men and women.

One assignment given to the students was to write and preach a sermon on a passage from Galatians. Three of the younger students were happy to announce that they had preached their sermons four times. They were a delight to watch, with neat haircuts and nice new suits that must have come from Germany!

I was able to visit one church service, and was pleased to see the men and women taking part in the questions and in reading the Word. The pastor brought Bibles for the people, as they did not have their own personal copies!

There was real love and caring between the pastor and the people. This pastor, one of our students, had eleven children and a colleague said he was the poorest man he has seen in the ministry in Russia. Yet, he was concerned about our every need. I was happy that we were able to give him gifts of coffee, sugar, soap, pencils, pens, tinned meat and Bibles!

Novosibersk differs from much of the rest of Russia, with the brightly painted wooden houses and long, cold winters. The people seemed proud of coming from Siberia, and loved their winters - .but with their fur coats and boots and hats they are well prepared for the cold!

May 23: Glamorous Travel

After flying back to Moscow we spent a cold rainy day hiding out in a hotel lobby, reading magazines and writing postcards. When the rain cleared, we walked through Red Square to Baskin Robbins to have ice cream for dinner.

Our train ride to Leningrad that night was not my favorite experience! I had never shared a tiny four bunk space with three men before - this was definitely not first class, nor even tourist, but second class. Phil kindly took his top sheet and made a little curtain over my bunk, but it was still uncomfortable. I wore ear plugs, but there was no way to avoid smelling the Russian man's shoes on the floor beside my bunk, or the smelly cheese and fish packed in his bag!

In the middle of the night, when the train stopped, I sat up and removed my ear plugs to hear the snoring of 3 men and I noticed that the big guy across from me had his pants on the floor alongside his jacket. It's a good thing I did not have to get up to go down the hall to the toilet that night!

Adventures are sometimes not dangerous, but just uncomfortable experiences.But none of it mattered as long as we got to teach more classes!!

May 24: Our Anniversary in Leningrad

We arrived in Leningrad at noon, in time for a meal and a long nap. The weather reminded us of Helsinki, Finland. There are only about 65 days of sunshine per year and we did not experience any of those special days!

Nothing was officially planned for our first day, but we had been given the name of a church and decided to visit. Arriving by taxi, we were welcomed, even though the service had already begun. We heard four preachers, four anthems, and many prayers during the several hours that we were there.

Before we knew it, some young English speaking women introduced us to the pastor and Phil ended up meeting with him and his staff. They had many needs, including questions about how to handle strife in the church. Over and over we hear the same questions!

Phil had them open the Bible and study the life of Paul. They also asked how to begin a Sunday school for children, and requested materials. As always, we encouraged them to produce their own, but helped them with some ideas.

With the help of a translator, the pastor's wife told me that she often felt that she had no faith left - she had felt that they were a forgotten people. But because of our visit she felt that she could believe God again. She confessed that she had asked the Lord to be able to meet *just one person* who had prayed for her country!

I realized afresh that *I represent a whole host of people who have faithfully prayed and cared for many years for her and for her country!* What a privilege it was to meet her. I guess the Lord knew that I needed to be encouraged. It *was* our wedding anniversary and she was God's gift of encouragement for us both!

The two young women accompanied us back to the hotel on public transportation, sharing their hearts with us. Both had been abandoned by their fathers and had grown up as third generation Christians, with parents living in exile. Life did not look too good to them and they wished to go to America as soon as possible.

One lived with her mother, brother, sister in law and nephew in a three room flat with three other families, sharing one bath and kitchen. Helen tried to leave the U.S.S.R. two years before, using an Israeli passport, even though she was not Jewish. She was stopped and had her passport taken away. Unfortunately, you need a passport to get a job!

A Congressman visited a year later and this small group of dissidents appealed to him for help. They received passports and visas to go to America anytime over the next three years. Helen was given a scholarship to a Methodist University in New York. She was worried that she might have a difficult time with her limited knowledge of English, but also believed it was God's way of helping her be able to eventually help her family.

Her mother, a teacher, lost her job, just as Helen did, when the government found out that they were Christian. Helen ended up working as a vegetable girl, selling potatoes in an outdoor stand. She was working to save the large amount of money needed for her trip to America, and lived on bread and potatoes only. When I gave her a large candy bar and some perfume and soap, she said she could sell them to add to her trip fund.

Her greatest burden was trying to make the church leaders understand her desire to leave. They did not understand how difficult life was for a single Christian woman: in the communal living situations, it was not uncommon for a woman like herself to be raped by the men, and so abortions are common as well. She said that she herself had 'experienced such things.'

We gave these women our address in the States and asked them to keep in touch. We would be praying for them!

Back at our hotel on our anniversary night we heard the same plea from our waiter – one of frustration and despair. He gave us a plate of cold cuts and Pepsi for supper, and told us that while it was good that American Christians visited his country, he wished that we could visit inside the people's homes to see how they really had to live!

He was thankful for his freedom but hoping for a leader who could be trusted to lead them throughout the hard transition the USSR must pass through.

One man told us, "Things are so much better than even five years ago, but one cannot think much about politics when there is not enough food to eat. Tourists eat and sleep very well, but for us meat and soap and material for clothes are rationed, and shoes are too expensive to buy. In July the prices are expected to triple due to another special austerity program. We do not know how we can manage: many will do the popular thing and commit suicide…"

As he spoke, I was reminded of Poland which had suffered a similar program of austerity. They *did* survive and things are better. Some folks did not realize that the Lord would lead them through! But others strongly trusted our Father.

I remember my parents' and grandparents' stories of life during the Great Depression. My own father worked several jobs at one time to provide for his family while training for the ministry. Some folks discover that times of hardship can offer a rich opportunity to see God at work….

But first - one has to hear of Jesus!

May 25: A Tourist Day

We had the opportunity to visit the Hermitage, possibly the most well known museum in Russia! In a two hour tour we were only able to see the main floor, even though the tour moved at a brisk pace - this place is gigantic, with the walls, ceilings and even the floors covered in gold and paintings. Huge chandeliers hang from the ceilings, eight and nine layers deep with crystal and gold, columns of gold and paintings from all over the world fill the space.

And yet the place was dirty and run down. I could not help but notice that many of the priceless paintings were hung in direct sunlight, and in need of cleaning... so unlike the museums we have been able to visit in Vienna.

We discovered that there was little we could buy with rubles. The gift shops all want dollars, even for a cup of coffee! We did manage to buy a cup of tea in a Russian hotel where they seemed pleased to serve us.

We were told that the waiters had to buy the food from the kitchen and then sell it to the customer....that may be why we saw a waiter take some uneaten food off one plate and put it on another!!

May 26: What the End of a Trip Looks Like!

We received our wake-up call at 2:30 a.m. to get up and onto a bus back to the airport. After a long wait at the airport we took off for

Moscow. A black Intourist agency car took us to the other side of the runway where we waited some more before our last flight took us home to Vienna!

It was mid afternoon when we arrived and we were so very tired that we allowed ourselves the indulgence of a taxi from the airport to our front door. We were just too tired to navigate the bus and the streetcar!! It was Saturday and all the shops in Vienna were closed so we were glad to have some bread and milk in our freezer.

Friends came, bringing us milk, fruit, and eggs as well as hugs and encouragement. It was so good to be warmly received! We looked through the mail and put clothes in the washing machine and then finally we slept!

We had over six weeks of steady responsibility and travel: Romania, Germany, the Soviet Union and then guests. We would have two weeks to rest before more guests would be on their way. Later we would travel to Czech, then Poland and then Romania again. Our summer is heavy with activities, and we pray for rest time in September. But always we remember why we do what we do!

Why Do We Do What We Do?

If ever we forget our reasons for all the travel and work, if ever we get discouraged, we have only to recall the responses we get from our students:

Nicolai: I have wanted to study God's Word from the age of 17 years. That was 13 years ago. I took one course without a teacher, but I had so many questions which went unanswered. I thank God that He has given me this class and it has strict rules to get me studying hard. I pray that I can continue for a long time.

Sergei: The Romans and Galatians course has meant a great deal to me in my personal life. It has helped us begin a Bible School for our people. We dreamed about such a school for a long time, but had no books or training. Now that you have come, we have 20 books in this subject and we can teach others. Pray that God will bless us and my brothers who sustain this ministry. My country needs this so much today. Thank you for coming to teach us! I pray for you!

Oleg: When I began reading these textbooks, I saw the great deal of work put into it. I think of the writers who worked so hard to make clear to me so many of my questions. I was so happy to have the teachers pray with me about the problems I face doing ministry. God gives me His grace. So many people want to study: I pray that I can use these studies to help them. Great is your reward for helping us to have these books!

Zoya: I have been studying the course with my husband. I have been a Christian since childhood, but while studying this course, I began understanding many things so much better. Now, I see that I can better answer the questions of unbelievers. These courses are not just for the pastors, but they are for all believers who want to be ready to tell others about Jesus.

Afanasy: I can compare studying God's Word seriously with eating a meal….you can eat simply or you can eat very richly! This course is eating richly! We have your help and challenge to use these materials and ideas in our sermons, in our everyday lives and in evangelism.

God's Word is real and it is real food for my hungry soul. Thank you for stirring us in our studies and in our teaching.

Despite the challenges of our time ministering in the USSR, we praised God for the harvest of souls and minds who responded to God's call in the seven years we have been here. God is so good and these were exciting years. We were always amazed by our students who had to work hard to carve out time for their studies, and who were so eager to teach others and pass on all that they learned. One example of that would be Irene…..

Where is Your God?

Irene had heard about a Bible study class being conducted in secret and she came to the church and sat outside the door to listen. Although she was not an approved student, her enthusiasm touched the hearts of the teacher and the students. Soon she was allowed to participate.

Our course of study at that time was Evangelism and Discipleship, and each of the students was required to share the gospel with others and report the results. Most of the students had places to preach or teach but Irene shared with me that she had found a ministry all her own and invited me to come see her in action.

Irene had grown up in Moscow in a Muslim family and had searched all her life for the truth about God. A stranger gave her a copy of the Scriptures, and as she read the Bible, God revealed Himself to her.

Irene dared to go to Arbat, a public square in Moscow, where people were allowed to get up on little platforms and recite poetry or give speeches. Irene used this place to share her faith in Christ. Many Muslims came to know Christ through her witness there.

The afternoon I went with her there was another woman who had come to the square to speak out. Greatly troubled; she carried a banner which said *I need help!* In the former days the square had been the place to look for help.

However, she found that no one in the government would listen to her. Many others in Russia felt as desperate as she did, only to commit suicide when they were repeatedly turned away.

Carrying her banner, she went looking for someone to talk to, when she saw a woman speaking to a crowd. She pushed her way to the front to hear Irene!

Irene talked about God and his love and care for people. This God she spoke of wanted people to follow Him. It was just too much for the woman who called out in a loud voice,"Where is your God? I need help!"

At first Irene was shocked, but she quickly realized that God was using this needy person to clarify His message through her. The woman's eyes were so full of hurt that Irene could barely look into them. She began to explain God's love for her and God's provision of His son Jesus Christ for the world.

Irene saw the woman's face soften as the Word of God touched her heart. She was thrilled to realize that through the Holy Spirit, God has the power to change the hearts, minds and lives of the people who hunger to know him.

Finally, the woman said, "Show me how I can have this gift of eternal life - I want to know God." Above the crowd, Irene and the woman began to pray. Soon many others in the crowd prayed to receive Christ as their personal Savior.

When the prayer was finished, and the woman started to leave, someone in the crowd picked up her banner to return it to her. "Here is your banner, you have forgotten it!" She replied… "I do not need it now: I have God, and I am going home to my family."

Have I ever doubted the power of God to change lives? Do I really believe He is the Almighty One? Irene has seen many miracles in her ministry with her people because she *expects* God to work and she is *obedient* to do her part.

Can I risk being misunderstood, being different, or being with hurting people for the sake of the gospel? How much do I really love people? Not just the cleaned up church crowd, but the needy, hurting and dirty people of the world?

God blessed Irene. She was even invited to share her testimony during the Billy Graham Crusade that came to Moscow that next year. She continues to share Christ with her Muslim people.

Irene's life helped me to see that God is powerful, sovereign, the Almighty One who reaches out to redeem His children throughout the whole world.

The Lord Jesus became the poorest of the poor, the loneliest of the lonely, and the most misunderstood one of all. Why?

So that we might know the loveliest of the lovely, the mightiest of the mighty, the one with power over death, hell and the grave. Jesus came to us so that we might know Him and have fellowship with God. God has promised to meet us at our deepest point of need.

"Come to me and I will give you rest…all who work so hard and carry heavy yoke   Wear my yoke for it will fit perfectly and let me teach you….For I am gentle and humble And you will find rest for your souls, For I give you only light burdens" Matthew. 11:28

PS When Irene shared her report to the class the next morning, the pastors had tears in their eyes…

CHAPTER FIFTEEN

Seeing Where We've Been

Matthew 19:29…."And everyone who has left houses or brothers or sister or Father or Mother or children or fields for my sake will receive a hundred times as much and will inherit everlasting life"

In 1994, Phil and I were once again afforded a new opportunity to serve on the staff with BEE International. While most people think about retiring when they turn seventy, we were back on the road experiencing the blessing of seeing places we had served and finding new places that needed Christ. We would eventually find ourselves in China, Vietnam and Burma serving in some of the most exciting ministries of our lives.

As we began this next leg of our journey, Jody Dillow, the world director for BEE wrote this to our soon-to-be coworkers at BEE.

> *The Smiths' were formerly associated with BEE International, which has changed its name to Church Leadership International and continues its leadership training in the countries formerly ruled by communists. BEE World is now a separate entity.*
>
> *As a staff member of BEE World, Phil will facilitate BEE training courses in China, Vietnam and in the U.S.; provide practical teaching and counsel in target countries, and write a Basic Pastors Training Manual for pastors in oppressed coun-*

tries.

Cindy will continue to minister to women in the target countries by giving training for leadership roles and speaking at women's retreats.

The Smiths will also continue follow-up ministry with their former contacts and friends in Russia and in Eastern Europe.

In June of 1995, Phil and I wrote a letter describing many of our experiences. It's hard to believe that we wrote this over twenty years ago.

Dear family and friends,

Thank you so much for praying. We were very conscious of Gods provision for our needs during this past trip. We traveled to new areas, experienced new challenges and opportunities and always felt His grace and strength.

We were also able to greet and encourage old friends. We had a wonderful time in Ukraine, Poland, Vienna and at the staff retreat at Berchtesgaden, Germany, Odessa, Ukraine:

Odessa

The travel arrangements went very smoothly, we marvel at being able to leave home in the early morning, in California to drive to the airport and arrive in Odessa, Ukraine all in one long day! It was 31 hours of travel before we were led to our bed at the seminary dorm in Odessa - .but oh that cot felt so good!

This is our first visit to Odessa. A seaport city on the Black Sea, Odessa once accommodated communist leaders as a resort. As we travelled through the city and countryside we saw little evidence of the infiltration of Western culture in this part of Russia. The economy has not yet changed since the fall of the communists.

The people are very poor, but the land and resources are rich. The farmers need equipment but small business opportunities abound. We saw an abundance of fresh vegetables and fruits, all from Turkey or Israel. Unfortunately, most people on the street cannot afford to purchase these beautiful goods.

We were impressed that the city was so clean and free from pollution from factories and steel mills. Nearly all the government factories are silent. There is plenty of dust and dirt, however, as the majority of the roads are not paved.

One thing we saw fascinated us: the streetcars and public phones are free! Crime was so prevalent after the fall of communism and without adequate leadership or policing no one could enforce the payment of the fees or prevent theft from the containers. So the leaders made a decree that they be free!

There are many reports of corruption in the new governments. Pray for them to find truth and respect and confidence in building a healthy government.

Pastor's Conference

Phil had a great time addressing the first-ever pastors' conference for lay pastors from the outlying areas who were not able to travel to the seminary program in Odessa. He loved hearing them sing and pray and interact.

We enjoyed being in Odessa during the Russian Easter celebration. The church was ecstatic at their first national holiday of Easter Sunday and Monday. Churches held services several times each day, keeping the Christians busy!

Ukrainian Wedding

At the close of a regular preaching service on Sunday morning we were delighted to witness a Ukrainian wedding. Four preachers delivered four long sermons! Finally the bride and groom walked to the platform where their parents were seated. The choir sang several songs, and the parents stood and prayed. With the translation we received, it sounded as though the wedding sermon was the entire marriage counseling course, given for the benefit of the church family.

After the ceremony, a single flower was presented to the bride and groom by each person in the reception line, along with the typical Russian kisses. Then we moved on to the reception hall where tables were spread with the first course of cold pickled dishes.

More speeches were followed by pictures and another course was served. After the tables were cleared there were more speeches and another course of food. We noticed that all the courses were served on the same small plates, and learned afterwards that they had to be washed and reused for each course!

It was nearly midnight when the bride and groom left while the rest of the family remained to clean up the hall.

Although the wedding made for a long day, Cindy found it a great opportunity to spend time with the children who were given a side room in which to eat and play. As the groom was from Yalta, many of the children had travelled from Yalta for the wedding and were cousins.

Ranging in age from 8-15 years old, many had studied En-

glish, but none had ever met a native English speaker. Cindy had a great audience! Some of them even begged to become a pen pal with her, telling her that they would receive a higher grade in their class work if they could write to someone in English. The children were all believers, but had no Sunday school - it was exciting to see that the parents had done a great job of teaching them the Bible.

Retreat for Women Missionaries

Another highlight for Cindy was her opportunity to address the first ever Intermission Women's Retreat, held in a villa right on the Black Sea. At one time it had been an elegant hotel for vacationing communist leaders. Despite the lack of heat and hot water, the women were so delighted to be together that having to huddle together in warm blankets during the messages did not seem to bother them at all.

The women had come from countries in the West as short term missionaries, to teach English in Russia and share Christ with these hungry people. For some of the women it was very emotional to hear hymns and choruses sung in English. Many had been in Russia for a year with no Western contact! Some were working in isolated areas in the Ukraine.

They had been spending their days studying the Russian language and adjusting to a vastly different culture. It was a great joy to be able to encourage these dedicated teachers! Thank you for praying - God was so faithful to give Cindy the right messages at just the right time.

Poland

After nine days in Odessa we were grateful to come back to Vienna and enjoy a nice, clean and warm hotel. We walked the familiar streets until we wore ourselves out and then went back to the hotel to nap and meet old friends for dinner.

The next morning we travelled all day by train across the corner of Czechoslovakia, noticing cleaner, brighter stations and signs in the small towns, painted houses and flowers everywhere. In the former, communist days, paint and flowers were considered symbols of materialism!

Arriving in Katowice, Poland, we were greeted by our dear brother Josef. We quickly saw the many big changes evident everywhere we looked. We saw tomatoes from Holland, oranges from Israel, and fresh greens and vegetables from Turkey in the street markets. No longer were there black market people hassling you on each corner.

The city seems so much more peaceful now. Even the people on the streets look much brighter in dress and expression. We did not see public drunkenness as in the recent past.

And yet, there is still fear; fear in the economy, fear in the government, fear in fear itself. There is opposition from the national church and many are not as interested in Christ, as material things now compete for their attention.

Once again we were reminded by our friends that persecution strengthens the church! There is a generation of younger people in Poland committed to making a difference in their nation: wanting to invite folks to turn from their culture and live for Christ.

Ustron: A Church is Born

We travelled to Ustron to spend time with the Wieja's and were *able to stay in the guest apartment of a medical building. The last time we saw this structure, it was run down with a huge hole in the backyard, and we took pictures of the ruins and prayed!*

What a thrill to see it now functioning as a medical center, with the most complete and modern laboratory in all of Poland, as well as a fitness center and a counseling center.

Dr. Henryk works full time in his medical practice to support the twelve nationals who do the 'work of the ministry'. Just five years ago, the Life and Mission Ministry came into existence. Usually, a church is formed first, and then various outreaches grow from that church. In Ustron, just the opposite happened! Many ministries came into existence as the first generation of believers began to develop and pursue their own individual ministry gifts: a prison ministry, youth ministry, children's ministry, women's ministry, leadership training, Bible institute ministry and even a publishing ministry. All began with just a dozen men and some committed women.

And now, after all these outreach ministries have grown, the foundation has been given a building by the Menlo Park Presbyterian Church in California in which to meet for worship. It is not yet called a church - but a place for the fellowship of believers.

Official permission still needs to be granted for a church, and there is opposition from the Catholics and Lutherans in the area. Henryk and Alina shared with us the persecution and trials of the past two years, surprising us when they said it has been more difficult than their struggles with the communist authorities. Even their 14 year old son has been beaten because of the faith of his father

We cried, laughed, hugged and prayed with them, promising their son Paul that if he came to America to study medicine, he could live with us.

Matthew 19:29….."And everyone who has left houses or brothers or sister or Father or Mother or children or fields for my sake will receive a hundred times as much and will inherit everlasting life….."

BEE Retreat

Then we were back on the train to Vienna to visit the new BEE office and meet the newest BEE staffers. This was an unusual gathering because never before had we accommodated so many families as they had moved 'in country'. There were special stories to be heard, hearts to be listened to, and folks to pray with.

During Skit Night it was great fun to see the mission kids perform. They are so gifted, yet so normal. Phil and I joined in, having slipped out secretly to put on wigs and change our clothes. No one recognized us as we began our skit!

After the speakers shared with us we had prayer time for each ministry and lots of time for sharing ways in which God has continued to bless our ministries!

Romans 11:33: "Oh the depth of the riches of the wisdom and knowledge of God! How unsearchable His judgments, and His paths beyond tracing out."

Joyfully His,

Phil and Cindy Smith

In November of 1995, Phil and I found ourselves back in Moscow, and could not believe the changes that had occurred in that city.

Phil and I had a Russian friend whose favorite greeting is, "I can't believe my eyes!" I found myself saying that over and over as I saw evidence of so many changes. In fact, there were so many changes that I insisted that my hostess, Carole, and my friend Natasha, go with me to Red Square on my last free evening of the trip. I wanted to make sure that I was truly in Moscow!

I found that even Red Square had changed. A cathedral had been rebuilt and the ancient gates restored. GUM, the old state run store, had become an expensive shopping mall. Even the old Revolutionary Square was under construction to produce a seven level underground Trade Center.

Changes were everywhere. At first glance the women at Passport Control at the airport appeared to be wearing the same old dull green uniforms, but then I noticed that their skirts were short and they were wearing fashionable shoes.

During our early days in Eastern Europe, we learned to pay attention to shoes. Certain government issued shoes were worn by all the important officials. Even if their dress seemed Western or casual, we were taught that their shoes would give them away!

Something definitely changed in the footwear in Moscow!

At the airport we found remarkable differences: more order and calm, no clamoring to exchange money and no fighting for a taxi. We were able to walk directly to a bus which took us to the Metro system.

Three years previous the State stores were dark and empty and people searched frantically for food. There were little kiosks on the streets and sidewalks, especially near the larger metro terminals. Now we found order, and the new striped tent-like Kiosks were removed every evening.

The huge state run stores of the past had become cooperative business ventures and were filled with everything you might need: American ice cream, frozen cakes, fish from Finland, and fruits and vegetables from south of Moscow. The only problem was the high prices!

Most of my friends and colleagues shopped at the outdoor markets where the prices are more reasonable. Shopping in Moscow still takes time and effort to find what you need. People were still hoarding things, so flour is beginning to disappear, as bread is the most important part of the Russian diet.

Fast food restaurants were everywhere with brightly lit signs advertising pizza and hamburgers, Chinese, Korean and even Mexican fare. New cars drove on greatly improved roads and even the sidewalks had been resurfaced. The orthodox churches were freshly painted and many of the old gray cement buildings had been resurfaced to look like colored marble.

My biggest surprise came when I met our old friends: it was so exciting to see that seeds planted in their lives years ago are growing and blossoming.

However, some had sad news to share. Our dear friend, Valentin, who was our driver and bodyguard during the difficult days of

1991 and 1992, shared that as a result of becoming a Christian, he had lost his wife and young daughter, as well as his apartment and money that he had invested. But he proudly held up his Bible, declaring, "But I have this!" He finds encouragement in all the changes in Moscow and has learned to depend on God for each day's work as an independent driver.

On a visit to our church I was delighted to find that the worship services are being conducted entirely in Russian. Two young men have been trained to take charge and they are excited about launching a new sister church this month. I wished Phil could have been with me to experience the warmth and love with which I was received as the church expressed their gratitude for the months of our service with them in their early days as a church.

One of the reasons for my trip was to spend time with Carole, who is working with Russian women to develop a Russian led small group network Carole's leaders have distributed over 500 invitations to friends and neighbors. Eight trained leaders have begun twelve Bible classes using a simple study curriculum on Joshua that Carole has developed. As most of the women attending the classes are not yet believers, the excitement runs high for the teachers and church leadership.

One highlight of my trip was attending a conference which gathered church leaders from all over the Soviet Union to discuss how to work together. This first meeting, called "The Gathering" was a chance for leaders to agree on a need for understanding and cooperation as they work together for God's greater glory.

One morning of the conference was given over to the older pastors who shared stories of their ministry during the dark years. An older pastor stood and with great emotion declared, "We older pastors have not had the training of you younger men, we were not allowed to go to the University or Seminary, because we were believers .But we *have* spent many hours with this book (he held up his Bible) and we know it! Many of us have spent time in prison and we do know how to pray!"

He asked us to help provide him with the training he needs to fulfill the ministry demands of today's world.

There was a quick burst of emotion when another older pastor rose to say that the younger churches were "stealing his chickens." A young man corrected him, "You mean to say stealing your SHEEP, not chickens." The laughter which followed help break the emotional mood!

But the older pastor's words began a conversation: there are churches springing up everywhere in Russia, both evangelical as well as orthodox. How long will it last? Will the Orthodox hierarchy clamp down again? The leaders reminded themselves that Russian history would suggest that we might only have a short time, so we must work as quickly as we can during these days!

God's goodness and promises were so evident on our return to Moscow. Little did we know God had an even great experience planned!

A Trip to Samara

God gave us opportunity after opportunity to follow His best plan for our lives. In 1996, we were able to visit Samara - a nineteen hour train ride from Moscow.

Listen to how Phil describes our trip in a letter her wrote to friends and supporters.

Dear Praying Friends;

Thank you so very much for your faithful prayers on our behalf. We have sensed the Lord's presence as we drove across the USA to the East Coast, then flew to Moscow and then a 19 hour train ride to the city of Samara.

As a military and communist stronghold, Samara has been a 'forbidden city' for visitors from the West since the days of Stalin. Samara is also the home of Luci, who became a believer while we were serving in Moscow. It was Luci who pleaded with us to come - wanting us to share the gospel with her family.

After three years of prayer about Luci's invitation, God began to reveal His plan for us to go, although we did not fully know what He had in store for us.

Last fall, while at a Moscow meeting of missionaries and pastors, Cindy met Benjamin Nesterov, a pastor from Samara. When she shared with him about Luci's invitation, Pastor Benjamin said, "Oh please come - we need help too!"

Victor Ryaguso, the senior pastor of the Transfiguration Baptist Church in Samara, issued us the necessary formal invitation for us to visit.

Luci and her husband Yuri met us at the Samara train station and took us to her parents' flat, where we would be staying. Although Luci's parents did not speak English, we enjoyed getting acquainted through sign language and gestures.

Opening photograph albums, they showed us pictures of their families and early life in Russia, and we brought out pictures of our family as well. John Maisel had given us copies of his tract, "Is Jesus God?" and they read it with us several times. Luci's mother said, "How can one be truly educated if she or he has never read the Bible?"

How amazing to be in Samara, a former communist stronghold, sharing the gospel in the home of non-believers, former communist party members! But love knows no boundaries and we knew we had some new Russian friends!

While in Samara, Phil was invited to address 25 new converts just before their baptism. The church is over 100 years old and currently about 100 people gather each Friday morning for prayer. We were surprised to learn that each pastor of this church has died in prison for his faith!

During our 30 days in Samara we were taken to visit smaller churches for weekday meetings. It is amazing how people will eagerly gather to hear a Western speaker! And it is always challenging to find out what our speaking topics will be!

One day Cindy had been asked to give her personal testimony, but as she was walking up to the platform the translator told her that the pastor had announced that she was to speak on two subjects; how a pastor can encourage his wife and how a pastor can raise Godly children!

She smiled at the pastor and asked him to prepare some questions for her as she finished. We later realized that it was the pastor to whom we had been sent to encourage and teach.

Two of the churches we visited were brand new and asked

for materials which I had been writing – "The Pastors Basic Training Manual." I spoke for several hours on subjects included in that study and was asked a few days later to read and correct any errors that the men might have made in copying my messages verbally. Once again we are reminded of how eager these men are for training. What a blessing to be a part of what God is doing there….if for only one month!

Pastor Victor serves as the Overseer of the 15 churches in the association with a true shepherd's heart. He asked us to find sister churches in America who could send over lay people for short periods, to help train Sunday school teachers, youth leaders, small group leaders and help staff summer camps. The pastor and other leaders would also like to learn English to be able to use more of the materials available to them.

We were able to travel to a camp site where young pastors were meeting to speak on Biblical marriage. Cindy challenged the men to invite their wives to learn alongside them. This was well received and they promised to pray for their wives and to include them in some of their many sessions.

Friends, we never know where God's path will lead us: we just keep our hearts and minds open to Him and study and worship at His feet. His path becomes clear in His time and in His ways!

Thank you for praying with us - we can't do this without you!

In Christ's love,

Phil and Cindy

PS Phil will be going to Vietnam in a few months – we can't say more just now. Pray!

CHAPTER SIXTEEN

Traveling the Asian Circuit

First Thessalonians 5:16: "Be joyful always, pray continually and give thanks in all circumstances, for this is God's will for you in Christ Jesus."

It is hard to express the joy and challenge we found serving in Asia at this point in our lives. I experienced God's presence through so many beautiful and needy people.

Listen to what Phil wrote to our partners in December of 1996, describing the particular challenges of ministry in Vietnam:

Dear Partners,

I have just returned from Vietnam where BEE World is training leaders for six different church groups. I greatly rejoice in the Lord that due to your prayers and support this trip was made a reality!

The church in Vietnam is a persecuted, suffering church, much as the Eastern European and Russian churches were. A pastor of an underground church told me, "The Communists killed my father when I was 6 years old. My brother served in the South Vietnam Army and was killed by the Viet Cong. When the Communists took over in 1975 I was put in prison for four years. I then went to Central Vietnam and started underground churches until it became too dangerous for me. I returned to South Vietnam and am starting churches here."

Many of the students in our classes are highly educated but have not had the chance to go to a Bible College or Seminary. They expressed great joy in our bringing Biblical training to them. One pastor told us that there has not been any Bible training in Vietnam since 1976! A Pastor's wife told us that our class is bringing her a "great peace" in her heart.

My translator said, "We have recently had persecution, our study together has helped us to be closer to the Lord. In the Galatians/Romans course we learned that the early church had much persecution. We know that God will give us strength for our times."

Each day I met one of the pastors at a certain place in the city and would be whisked away on the back of a motorcycle to some secret location to meet with a group that formed our class for that week.

I have so many more stories which I want to share - but it must wait until the next letter. Please pray for these new classes and what our involvement might be. Burma is the next country we have been asked to check out for beginning new classes there. Pray!

In Christ's love,

Phil

What a blessing to be able to bring training to so many talented and committed pastors! Phil had many powerful experiences of God's protection and provision. We truly worship a God who provides.

Just hours before Phil left for Vietnam, the realtor told us that our

California condo had sold. Phil left the next day for Vietnam and I left for New Mexico to speak at a retreat for women in the Air Force. What a joy for us to get that news!

Phil's two weeks in Vietnam were heart-warming and meaningful. For the first time in BEE's ministry, they were able to present each student with a certificate for completing five of our study courses. Phil and the others were so proud to recognize their hard work with certificates with endorsements from BEE WORLD, and the Dallas Theological Seminary Center for Biblical Studies.

In a letter to supporters Phil, wrote, *"You should have seen the joy and happiness of these men! I wish you could have seen the smiles on their faces; they were so pleased with their accomplishments."*

Phil experienced the power in prayers throughout his trip. Early one morning he was riding on the back of a motorcycle, behind his trusted driver when another motorbike came up beside them. He felt a thud on his back and realized that the other driver had hit him. Phil's driver explained that the man was trying to steal Phil's shoulder bag.

But God protected Phil: he was carrying his Bible, teaching notes, passport, visa, and money in that bag! He knew in that moment that people were praying.

A little later, an on-coming truck swung out in the road to pass a group of motorcycles. In doing this, he veered to his left, forcing Phil to the edge of the road and he went down.

Putting out his hand to break the fall, he skidded along the pavement with his entire weight supported by his left hand. When he came to a stop with the motorcycle on top of him he was afraid to look at his hand. Not only were there no cuts, scratches or bruises, but he was not injured in any way - except for a tear in his sock!

The pastors in Vietnam experienced increased persecution from the Communist security police and asked Phil to tell brothers and sisters in America to pray for them, which he did in many prayer letters sent to the states.

Listen to what Phil wrote in September 1998.

> *While in Vietnam last May, I met a dynamic young pastor, Moses, (not real name) who was our BEE Pastor training class leader. Moses and some other students travel often to the tribal countryside in Vietnam to do evangelism and plant churches. Moses also joins together with another student, Aaron, to drive by motorcycle every month to Hanoi to conduct evangelistic services.*

> *Because they rent a Catholic hall for their services, the Communist authorities do not seem to bother them, assuming that it is just another Catholic service. A former Viet Cong army colonel has accepted Christ as his Savior and has started a church. When Moses is in Hanoi, he visits this colonel and trains him in ministry, using the BEE materials that he has studied. This is only one of the many exciting stories of our BEE trained pastors, and the far-reaching effect of their ministries. Your prayers and financial investment makes training possible for men like Moses!*

Eventually, Phil and I would serve in Vietnam together, but first we were called to serve the people of Myanmar (Burma). Our time in Burma included so many God moments it's impossible to put them into words!

In a letter Phil wrote upon our return from Myanmar, Phil expressed beautifully our experiences and our gratitude for the prayers of those who supported us.

Dear Friends,

We have just returned from Myanmar and are so grateful for your prayers. We experienced the Lord's care; especially when the plane made a stop and we got off only to discover it was not the right stop. We had to scramble to get back on! God's grace and patience were also felt when I needed to teach for two days before the students' study materials could get printed!

We fell in love with the gracious, fun loving, and caring Burmese people! One of the first things we noticed was the distinctive dress: both men and women wear long wrapped skirts. The men wore western shirts or tee shirts and the women wore blouses. The footwear is very practical, given that it is monsoon season; everyone wears simple thong sandals. The women, however, set themselves apart by wearing a paste made from bark to protect their skin from the sun. Worn on their cheeks, like rouge it is considered very beautiful.

We enjoyed great hospitality during our trip, although we had to get accustomed to being the objects of much curiosity! Outsiders were not common in the areas we visited so we got used to being stared at!

Burma is a very poor nation, having been held back by their military dictatorship. Shortages of electrical power occur almost every day. It has been a 'closed country' for so long that we were asked many questions about the world outside, about other believers in other places and about our own families.

Over 175 years ago Adoniram Judson gave his life in an effort to spread the gospel in Burma, and he is still considered a 'saint' here. Yet many of the schools, hospitals and mission compounds established by his ministry are under the control of the government. There is a statue of Judson in a prominent place here, but not many know his connection with Jesus!

But there is one group which is thriving and has a plan to reach this generation for Christ. The Chin tribe of Burmese invited us to come and teach them. What a joy it was to see an old Anglican-style church still being used for worship. Badly in need of paint and repair, it is being used to share Christ, in a compound of bamboo houses.

During a meeting Cindy asked several of the women to share how they came to faith in Christ. Many came to Christ through direct evangelism, having heard the gospel from a Burmese evangelist in a tent meeting. Some were able to travel to India to study at a Presbyterian Bible school and come back to work in the churches here. One of the women, inspired by Adoniram Judson, is working in a remote area, translating the gospel into a tribal language.

In my journal I wrote,"What kind of legacy will I leave my children and the people with whom God has asked me to share Christ?" I ask you the same question as you labor alongside us as prayer supporters and financial supporters, because we are in this together!

Phil and I were inspired and touched by so many people in Myanmar.

On a different trip to Myanmar, we were to plan a Pastor's Conference and a Women's conference along with teachers sent by the

BEE World office. After our long trip from Colorado Springs to Yangon and three days in Yangon, we flew to Mandalay to find that the temperature was in the 100's with the humidity about the same! We felt blessed to be housed in a hotel with air conditioning!

The women came for the meetings from eight different Burmese tribes, many having traveled for two days in the back of a truck to get to Mandalay. The tribes have historically been in conflict with each other so it was a touch of heaven to observe the unity that these 140 Christian women had with one another. The Holy Spirit was ministering to all our hearts!

In one session, I asked some of the ladies from various tribes to give their personal testimonies. We learned that the Chin tribe is mostly Christian and is dedicated to reaching the whole tribe by the turn of the century. Many of the women came from a Buddhist background and wish to reach other Buddhists with the gospel.

A large tent was erected next to the Judson Memorial church as a dormitory for the women, while the pastors slept on the church floor. Sessions were from 8:00 a.m. to 5:00 p.m, and the men met outdoors under the bamboo trees.

A woven bamboo shed served as the Bible school chapel and dining room, and we were fortunate to have a gentle breeze most of the time. 130 men, all pastors or pastors in training were taught, and the police did not bother anyone, as the meetings were under the sponsorship of a long accepted church in the community.

Plans were drawn up for more training and teaching in other areas using BEE materials, on the Seminary level. There is such a hunger for Bible teaching here: when we were visiting the pastors' homes we noticed people taking notes, and they asked us many questions about how to lead groups. As a child, Phil would pray for Burma: he expressed so much joy at being able to serve in ministry there.

Going to Vietnam as a Team

After returning from Myanmar, we were excited to be able to travel together to Vietnam to teach a marriage class. What a joy to visit the places where Phil had been. I looked forward to experiencing this new country!

Although we had initially been hesitant about teaching this course on marriage, fearing possible cultural problems, the response was incredibly positive. Many of the pastors had entered arranged marriages with well educated women who were expected to support the family. In many of the families, the grandmothers did the cooking and provided child care.

When we asked the men how they knew their spouse was God's will for their lives we learned that for most pastors in Vietnam, older pastors would play a large role in choosing a wife for them. The older pastor would begin looking amongst churches for a godly family with daughters. The young pastor would meet first with the young woman's parents and if all agreed that it was a suitable match - and it can take years to come to this agreement- then the couple meet. The young woman would need to experience a strong calling to be a pastor's wife, as it could be a very dangerous life!

We were blessed to able to take part in the first graduation from this course. And as always, it was both gratifying and eye opening to hear the comments and responses of our students. Let me share some of those now:

Pastor H: *The emphasis on communication has helped us improve the atmosphere in our marriage. We now understand each other and can speak more clearly what is on our hearts. Before, when we had conflicts, we kept silent. Now, we have learned to resolve our problems together - we do not criticize one another and feel like we are on a honeymoon, taking time to cherish each other.*

From T: *I know now, how to love my wife. I must love her unconditionally as my Lord loves me. I pray to God to help me do so…in order to obey Him and to bring happiness into my home. I thank God for the professors who came to teach this course.*

From LKH: *This BEE course has been so valuable and practical for me. I wish to thank those who wrote this course and traveled so far to teach us. We are now able to upgrade our personal ministries with a strong family life and relationship with our partner.*

The leaders who were behind the initial invitation for us to come to Vietnam asked us if I would come and teach this course just to the women. It was decided that if I would teach at a different time than the men's classes, it would be safer and not disrupt the families as much. It was also suggested that Phil not come each time and that at times he should bring 'tourists' with him, and they would go sightseeing while I slipped away to teach. We had to take many precautions in order to keep our teaching secret and keep our brothers and sisters in Vietnam safe!

From Cindy's Journal: 1999

Here's a look at how God was using me - from my journal:

Back in the USA a friend and colleague contacted me about becoming a part of his travel business as a cover for my trips. So I became a staff member of Friendship Tours, and despite minimal advertising, God provided 5-6 people for each trip to serve as a 'cover' for me. One of our pastors was a travel agent and helped me keep my 'tourists' busy.

I am certain that each "tourist" who saw Vietnam during those days was stretched in their faith and walk with the Lord. Most of the groups would take some of our pastor/students and their families out for dinner at small restaurants. It was a big blessing for their children to be able to practice speaking English, and to realize that there were Christians in America who cared for them and prayed for them.

One tourist group came from Seoul, Korea and they prayed around the clock for our students. Because of their prayer support I saw God do some wonderful things in my classes.

Now, years later, some of our leaders' children are grown and have made their way to the USA for schooling and are serving our Lord all around the world. God has given me grandchildren everywhere I go!

Often our "tourist" would look up villages and find where they were adopted. One hotel hosted a dinner for my guests who had found relatives in a nearby village. For a long time I received invitations from the Tourist Bureau of Vietnam, inviting me to bring friends and to check out a new tourist attraction.

Back home in Carlsbad, CA. Phil was working towards his D Min studies. His desire was to create the most helpful studies for the men he had met around the world. Often he would bring his work to a pastor and ask if this was what was needed. He was touched by their delight in his prepared studies for them. Many of the classes were developed out of a personal need that one pastor had. Phil was a father figure to many of our students, full of love, but still willing to warn them of personal habits or problems which he thought might hinder them.

Our women's classes grew, and other American women fell in love with teaching these women. Soon a BEE Women's Ministry to Vietnam was developed and our students followed the BEE requirement of teaching what they had learned to others. One of the students from the first BEE class was fulfilling this requirement by developing a ministry serving those living with HIV, leprosy and other illnesses. This woman had gone up North to some land behind a city dump to develop a ministry village. She collected wood from the dump and began building cottages.

Up on the nearby mountain she found people who were left to die and brought them down to her village, giving them each a job. As each would come to know Jesus, she gave them responsibilities and duties as their health would permit. You could not find a happier, sweeter village anywhere in the world.

One dear old man was blind and was given the job of keeping the music going in the village. Children with faces badly deformed from leprosy were taught to sweep the earth roads. There were flowers in flower boxes, and bells in the bell tower in the little chapel.

Some of the residents had the job of going around each morn-

ing to open the wooden shutters of the cottages for those who couldn't do so for themselves. There were gardens and communal kitchens and laundries where everyone was happily at work-slowly but ably.

My visit to this village was secret, to keep the village itself a secret from the government. The pastors who drove me and my two friends there on motorbikes were deeply touched. When we heard the leader of the village explain how difficult and exhausting her life had become, the pastors promised to assist this dear sister in her ministry. I was thrilled to see that our Father had a bigger plan than just me seeing what one of my first students had done with her teaching!

You Know You Are in Vietnam

As I reflected on my time in Vietnam, I wrote a piece called, "You Know You Are in Vietnam When,' to help my friends and family understand our experience. I hope you enjoy.

You Know you are in Vietnam when:

A hot breeze hits you as soon as you leave your air conditioned hotel, and your "contact person of the day" meets you at the appointed spot and takes your bag with your study notes as you climb on the motorbike behind the driver. You put your feet on the footrest and find the strap to hold onto, secure your hat and sunglasses, and off you go!

You know you are Vietnam because you have a skilled driver who weaves in and out of traffic so closely that you could reach out and touch a nearby biker, but you need your arms and legs so you tuck yourself in tightly!

You know you are in Vietnam when you peek ahead of the driver and marvel at the sight of a cart full of lumber being propelled by a man on a bicycle, a truck trying to weave through the motorbikes, a car filled with nervous looking tourists, and two people with pails on poles trying to cross the busy street.

You know you are in Vietnam when you turn the corner to see a busy outdoor market with all kinds of fruits, vegetables, flowers and freshly cut meat! Your driver stops to buy onions and hands them to you to carry in your lap. You realize this was all done because he thinks you are being followed.

Suddenly, there is a stop, and your driver pushes you lightly to exit with your onions - he tells you to be quick! He will bring your Bible and materials…You can hear the soft music of women singing and so you know you are where you are supposed to be.

You know you are in Vietnam, because on the other side of the gate you will take off your shoes and jacket and be greeted with hugs and kisses and the biggest smiles!

You know you are in Vietnam when the students beg to sit on the cool marble tiled floor rather than the plastic chairs. They prefer to do their exams on that floor and kneel to pray there. Amazingly, that floor gets a swipe of a scrub cloth when it is time to eat, and then becomes a sleeping place, before classes begin again!

Often after the nap, time is given over to hearing personal stories and prayer requests. You learn which families had Bibles and study materials confiscated, houses searched and children frightened. You pray with them about teenagers who don't want Christ because of the persecution they see their parents undergoing. You are touched when you hear that the children of pastors are denied access to schools of higher learning.

You know you are in Vietnam, when you hear a woman tell of having her motorbike and Bible taken away by the local police the night before the class. She tells you that her husband found someone to bring her to the city and she has no money or Bible or way to get home. You smile when the ladies pray for her and for the police who took her bike and Bible. She says, "I am learning about the character of God, He is Sovereign and he will make this situation work out for His glory and good. I am encouraged to trust Him even more."

You know you are in Vietnam when at the very next class you learn why the woman's bike was taken away. It seems another pastors' wife who had not been selected to take the course had told the police where our student was going. So the police confiscated her bike, but when she got home she found the bike had been returned. The police reported that the other pastors' wife had confessed to them that she had lied and was jealous. The police only remarked how 'ugly some women can get over a trip to the city'! And the jealous wife is now being discipled by our student!

From Cindy in 1999: A "Thank You Journal"

I had so many circumstances in Vietnam that drew me closer to our Father in Heaven. Not that everything was good, but God has the ability to bring good in all situations for those who love Him and seek to follow Him. I would spend my mornings writing in a "Thank You Journal" to help me see just how God was working. Here's a sample from Vietnam:

> *Today I thank you Lord for providing safety for me in the class in an upstairs room of the church. When the police came downstairs we were warned and I was scurried off to a tiny bathroom to wait while the police came upstairs to find only a 'birthday party' for one of the women! How creative these women were and how well prepared for a possible visit from the enemy.*

> *Thank you Lord for letting me see the love and compassion in my students today. One student arrived a day late sharing how the police had taken away her Bible and her family was so fearful when she came to class. It was beautiful to see the ladies as they held her and prayed for her. Thank you for letting me feel their love and passion for studying these subjects.*

> *Today Father it was great fun when my partner Barb and I stopped for a treat at an ice cream shop in downtown Saigon. It just so "happened" that as we were trying to figure out the menu and asked if anyone spoke English, one lady stood up and offered her services! Of course it was the leader of one group of our students, and all around her were 17 students who were about to order ice cream too! What fun it was to treat these ladies to a first visit to an ice cream store in downtown Saigon, before they left two by two to return to their villages.*

> *Today I thank you for allowing me to hear the testimony of one pastors wife: she shared that her son had come home and*

apologized for his rudeness and started back to church. When his father asked what caused the sudden change, he said that although his Buddhist girlfriend and her family were fun loving and he enjoyed being in their home it seemed like his own family had changed after taking the BEE marriage course. He felt like his parents were happier and more interested in their family and not as 'caught up in ministry.' So he had decided that he would be happier at his own home now. Wow! Thank you Lord for showing me this result!

Today I thank you for sparing my life during the tumble off the motorbike! Although I am concerned for my driver who had to seek medical treatment for a cut, I know that the bike landed just a couple feet from the truck wheels and my head was right there! Thank you for protection and peace!

Vietnam - October 2000

The last assignment we gave our class in Vietnam required our students to study the spiritual gifts and ask God how He might want to use them and their gifts. It was fascinating to hear their reports!

Rachel reported this to us:

I am married to a pastor in a tribal area, but since I married early in life, I had no opportunity to study the Bible. As I talked to the Father about this assignment, this is what He told me to do.

I took my motorbike to a nearby village which has not yet heard the gospel. At first I walked and prayed, asking the Lord to show me what He wanted me to do: I knew He had directed me here.

I found a poor family, who lived in a bamboo lean-to built against another house. Their little boy was blind and I began reading Bible stories to him. Soon his parents and a few others with children came to hear the stories read in their tribal language. Somebody told the chief of police what was happening, but it turned out that the house where the lean- to was built was his home!

He soon came to listen, hanging his hammock on the back wall of his bamboo house so he could hear what I was saying. He told the people that he heard nothing against the government, and asked me if his brother could come listen to the stories.

The next time I visited I brought my husband who became friendly with the policeman and invited him to church: He came to church and received Christ as Savior.

Dramatically changed, the policeman stopped drinking and beating his wife, and even burned the idols in his house. Although his wife liked the changes, she was afraid of living without the idols in her home! She came to our meetings but each time she had terrific headaches. Soon I discovered that she was the chief sorcerer in her village, which was deeply influenced by witchcraft.

Our church prayed over the policeman's wife and cast out a demon, enabling her to be able to receive Christ! Soon she and her husband led their children and two other couples to Christ.

Although the policeman lost his job, the men of his village respect him so much that they protect him and all the new believers from the government.

Rachel was such an encouragement to the women in the BEE class. One of the frustrating things the government is doing in the tribal areas is building houses for the poor only if they keep an idol in a prominent place in their home. It is thought that the government is afraid of losing their control over these people.

Tabithia reported:

> *In our area the government tries to keep the old customs which makes it difficult to share the gospel. One member who received Christ changed drastically when he left behind his alcoholism and began burning idols in an open pit. Everyone in the village noticed and the government responded by driving him out of his home and refusing to let him work in the village. Despite this persecution, his faith is strong and he is being used by the Lord.*

Elizabeth reported to us:

> *My husband, when I married him, had a very small church. Now it has grown from 20 members to 700 members, most of them new believers! I am responsible for training each new believer.*

> *We have no problems with the government just now, because the government official in our area has become a believer! When the new believers tear down their idol altars it becomes a public announcement that they have decided to follow Christ. But once that decision is open, our church steps in to encourage and lift the new believers up. When any of our group face persecution we band together to face it.*

> *We also run a school for the blind, deaf and dumb, across the street from the church. The government has given us permission to have this: in fact they have asked us to teach sign language and we do it with Bible stories!*

Jeremiah 33:9 Then it shall be to Me a name of joy and praise and an honor before all nations of the earth, who shall hear all the good that I do to them……

How I Met My Husband

In each of our women's classes, we require the students to write their personal testimonies and share them with the class.

One student shared with us: "How I Met My Husband"

From childhood until the age of 16 I lived in a Catholic convent in Vietnam, and was about to take vows to become a nun. My parents had to agree to sign the papers, and they were willing to do so, but my grandmother disagreed and there was much angry discussion!

However, the problem was solved when the government took over the convent in 1975, forcing the missionaries to leave. I went to live with my grandmother and entered a rebellious period of my life. My parents did not seem to want me in their lives and I got into lots of trouble. I felt that I was ugly and that boys would never be interested in me. My family was so messed up that not even the girl students liked me. At 16, I felt my life was just a big nothing.

I was still a Catholic, however, and was allowed to go to church. In some way I felt loyal to the church which showed me love and seemed to care about me.

At the time many goods were rationed in Vietnam and I was caught making illegal copies of ration papers at the University. I went to meetings of students who were angry and trying to find ways to cause mischief with the University or the govern-

ment.

Sometimes I would not go to class or to my part time job. Yet my grandmother continued to be an encouragement to me, protecting me from the consequences of my rebellious actions.

I remember having a dream that I would finish my university studies at HCMC and do well. That dream helped me believe that I could do something meaningful, so I asked for permission to live on campus and was shocked when I received it!

I was happy in the University housing. I had a roommate who read her Bible openly and invited me to a secret meeting with a pastor and students. I always liked things that were done in secret! I went to the Protestant meetings and then to the Catholic Church to confess that I was going to the Protestant meetings! Finally, the priest said to me, "You need to make a decision which church you will belong to"

When I spoke to the Protestant pastor, he explained the gospel to me as well as the differences between Catholic and Protestant beliefs. He emphasized that I must make a decision, and it would affect the rest of my life!

With my roommate, I prayed and accepted Christ as my Lord and experienced a great peace within myself and also with others and with God!

Then I developed a tumor in my neck. When the doctors gave me medicine it made me sick. I asked God to heal me and in a dream I felt the Spirit of God touch me and tell me that I would be healed. When I told the doctor about the dream and informed him that I was going to stop the medicine he said, ""Do what you wish but don't you ever ask me for medication again!" My Christian friends prayed with me and that tumor slowly disappeared.

I met my husband at a youth Bible study. He seemed very nice and was handsome, but he didn't talk much. One day when I saw him talking to another woman at church my heart fell and I knew then that I had deep feelings for him. When he later asked me to go on a motorbike ride with him I was very happy!

But he had some serious problems: his father was in prison for making copies of Bible teaching materials. My husband protested and was put into prison for one year. After his release he was once again caught making copies of Bible materials.

He told me he needed to see how serious his legal situation was with the police. He wanted to try a test, to see if he was on the suspect list for more prison. It was only a test, he said, because no marriage certificates were issued to people in trouble. I agreed to sign the paper to apply for a marriage license with him – just as a test!

When I told my grandmother, she was furious with me, explaining that any such paper was indeed legal. I was now indeed married to this man - it was NOT a test! She was very concerned because no one wanted their daughter to marry a pastor, especially when his father was already in prison. Grandmother was afraid my parents would cause trouble....all because of my insensitive and impulsive actions.

My roommate showed great concern and care for me and my grandmother. She arranged for my husband-to-be and his mother and brother to meet with my grandmother. My grandmother liked them all very much, especially my husband! The papers had been approved! He was not in trouble with the police as the last policeman did not file any reports about him.

The family of this dear woman decided to set a wedding date in 6 months. So her wedding certificate shows her date to be 6 months before the actual ceremony. She has now been married 13 years and together with her husband has been serving a church. They valued the marriage course very much!!

While we were serving in Asia, we were given many opportunities to bring God's word to people who desperately longed to receive it and share it with others. Knowing the word built the strong foundation they needed to stand against the Communist regime that desperately sought to discourage and dismantle Christian churches.

Below, I share with you a personal note I wrote as I reflected on my time bringing God's word to the people of China.

Bibles to China!

I praise God for the opportunity to carry His word to hungry hearts. During my recent "delivery" ministry trip to Hong Kong and China, I saw our Father at work in so many ways! Being told that each piece of literature carried in is studied by at least 20 people makes even the heaviest deliveries become lighter!

Trusting our Father at each border crossing (up to four times a day), I saw God blind the eyes of custom officials, distract them or cause confusion. My greatest joy was to see the look on the face of our Chinese contact when he would receive the books. His job is so dangerous: I pray for the safekeeping and storage of these books inside China.

Another great joy was attending BEE training classes and meeting the Chinese students using those books. I was amazed to learn how many congregations they serve! I saw copies of the delivered materials, including a small tract I had published in Hong Kong and carried through the border to our contact.

Seeing that tract, in Chinese, in their hands, I quietly praised the Lord that we could have a small part in equipping these servants in a very practical way.

There is a factory in China, where people gather at midnight to secretly make small souvenir magnets in the shape of the map of China. In English and in Chinese, the magnets say, "pray for China." Inside the usual insignia of China, they have boldly placed a tiny cross. The believers slip them into the hands of visitors coming to China.

God is at work in China! Although the opposition at every level is very strong, the believers are courageous. I think of their struggle as a pinprick of light inside a dark tunnel. And yet the light does prevail – praise God!

"For it is the God who commanded light to shine out of darkness, who has shone in our hearts to give the light of the knowledge of the glory of God in the face of Jesus Christ."

II Corinthians 4:6

CHAPTER SEVENTEEN

Retirement: Already?

"He makes me lie down in green pastures, he leads me beside quiet waters, he restores my soul."

When Phil wrote up a letter of retirement to give to BEE World, I was shocked as I still enjoyed teaching in Vietnam. After talking and praying, Phil asked me to write out a list of what I would like to do over the next fifteen years if the Lord continued to give us good health.

I was not too surprised that Phil had already spent some time creating a 'bucket list' of goals and objectives. For many years we kept a little fish bowl in the kitchen filled with ideas we had written down for a day out, and we would take turns selecting from the bowl.

One such "day out" I will never forget: It had been Phil's turn to select the outing and he told me it was a surprise and I needed to pack us a lunch. I thought it meant a hike or a trip to the beach, so I packed some sandwiches and we hopped in the car. Once in the car, we drove, and drove, and drove until we found ourselves at the Riverside Military cemetery!

I laughed so much that Phil had to tell me to stop and be more respectful. While eating our lunch Phil told me that he had made arrangements for us to be buried in this place. He wanted me to not be afraid of coming here, when the time came, thinking that if I was familiar with the place, it would relieve some of the anxiety. How wise he was!

So on Phil's bucket list was more travel, to visit and encourage leaders in the countries we had served. He wanted to revisit Poland to see what life and ministry was like for our dear friends. He wanted to visit our dear ones in Australia…Ros and John and their family. All our married life he had spoken of his days during World War II in the Philippines and he wanted to visit friends in ministry there.

First Stop: The Philippines

We decided to attend a BEE WORLD International conference in the Philippines and then continue on to visit Phil's friend Jim who invited us to minister to a group of pastors and their wives who had never had any formal training.

After the ten days of teaching, we were asked to perform a Christian wedding ceremony, as the couples had never had a ceremony, even though many had been married for years. We were confused because we hadn't even spoken about marriage in our classes. Back at Jim and Shonda's apartment I noticed a Marriage Manual that Jim had written, which had marriage vows - once again, the Lord provided just what we needed, just when we needed it!

So the next day after presenting graduation certificates, we began a group wedding ceremony only to find out that each couple wanted their own individual service! We spent the afternoon and evening leading these precious couples in their vows, with lots of pictures and prayers and tape recordings.

Phil enjoyed being taken by our hosts to the beach where he had first given his life to the Lord at the age of nineteen. Although his body was weak, he tried to swim but he missed the waves which usually helped propel him.

The List Continues

After the Philippines, Phil wanted to visit a young couple who had been in a Bible study with us in Carlsbad, and who now lived in Macedonia, ministering with the Albanians. After that, we wanted to find some of the people on his extensive prayer list. Many were new believers in the military whom he was encouraging while others were new leaders in far away countries.

His bucket list went on and on: to grow a beard, find a C-melody saxophone and play again, buy some sweaters for California beach living. He wanted to prepare a guest room for visitors from other countries, wanting to make sure that children, whose parents were international church leaders, would be welcome in our home while they were studying in America.

And finally, Phil wanted to spend time with our grandchildren, building relationships with them. We had missed so much time with them while we had been working around the world with BEE.

When Plans Change

In July of 2005 we had a bad auto accident in the mountains just above Palm Springs. Phil had taken some cold medication and gotten sleepy and we went off the road. After hitting fences and trees, we came to a stop, with the car turned on its side up against a rock. God provided emergency service before we could even call. A wildfire was burning in the area and the fire department was already in the area. God was there all the time!

After a year of healing, we celebrated Phil's 80th birthday, with a big gathering of family and old and new friends. We surprised him with a picture book of the first 25 years of his life, and family telling some of the stories of those years. Phil's favorite gospel musician, Chuck Butler, entertained; performing a song he had written for Phil (you can read the song at the beginning of the book). Phil said over and over how much fun it was to be awake at your own wake!

It was at this time that Phil's doctor began noticing some changes in his health. He was becoming confused and anxious if I was not around. For me it was a struggle as I had to have several surgeries for injuries from the accident.

After I had healed somewhat, our church in Danville invited us to be guests on their cruise to the Holy Land. Cruising with a gathering of close friends was a tremendous gift. It was great to see the many changes in that part of the world and to enjoy our friends along the way

We were back home, preparing for another surgery for me when

Phil's doctor called me into his office to tell me that Phil had Alzheimer's disease, and recommended that we find a specialist. When my own doctor asked about my high blood pressure just hours before my surgery, I told him about Phil and he promised to help find the best doctor to care for Phil.

And just a few days after the surgery we received a phone call from a wonderful, godly Messianic Jewish doctor, Dr. Kaveh Farhoomand, who asked us to come for a visit. At his office, we were warmly greeted and at once we both felt peace: once again God had provided just what we needed!

After tests and many discussions we agreed to his total care of both Phil and me. He led us through almost three years of caring for Phil in our home. His coaching was a huge blessing and the hospice workers he sent were all believers, which was a great blessing.

Making Final Plans

In the last five years of Phil's life, he began preparing for his home going. With our son Danny's help, he cataloged his collection of books, and sorted through nine boxes of trip reports and journals. He wanted to publish a book with me about our 'adventures in marriage,' to be a gift to our children and supporters who stood faithfully beside us throughout our journey.

One of his files which I found interesting, was one I had not seen before, called, "Words of Encouragement" Phil had saved everything, from Fathers day cards, thank you notes and even words of correction from church parishioners. In some places he had circled an area, noting that this part was true, and another section was

FALSE!

Another component of this file was the testimonies and words that encouraged_his heart which you'll find in Appendix #1.

Last Days with Phil

Phil's testimony was strong up until the very last days that he could speak. He shared with the young man who came to fix our AC. This young fellow had recently gotten out of prison, where he had received Christ. Now, he was searching for the fellowship that he missed while in prison. Phil invited him to come along to a gathering of guys at our church....which he did.

Phil also shared his life and many stories with the hospice workers who came night and day to care for him. He was so grateful for the volunteers who came to walk with him or to visit out on our patio. Phil was grateful to the very last breath.

He kept his sense of humor too! Once as I was bustling through the house doing chores, he called out to me. I went to see what he wanted, and he said, "Will you marry me?" Of course I was thinking about the "shoes in the closet" proposal, and I told him, "I am much too busy right now taking care of an old friend - I will get back to you soon!" For several hours that day, he repeated that same request.

His hospice nurse read scripture passages to him, as did I. He loved hearing scripture read out loud and told me that he wished churches today would do that. He said that seeing it on the 'overhead' was not the same for him. Hearing it read out loud is a rich experience!

I promised Phil that I would indeed 'finish my race well', and I would look for what God wanted me to do after he was gone. I know that I was blessed to have lived for 60 years with this man who was God's intended gift for me. The prayers of my family and his were answered when God brought us together. I can see back through the years how through each and every difficult situation, God was at work, forming me to be what Phil needed and to be ready for what God had planned for us to accomplish together.

In September our son Joey and his wife Audra and our grandchildren, Joshua and Kate, arrived to celebrate Phil's 86th birthday. Phil enjoyed so much the company of Joshua and Kate. They helped push Gramps in his wheel chair and walked beside him when he used the walker. Kate loved to sing for her Gramps, and he taught her "You are My Sunshine," which she still sings in his memory. One night when her daddy was visiting and she was back home in San Clemente preparing for bed, she asked Gramps, over the phone, if she could sing with him and say his bedtime prayer! He smiled at the sound of her voice - the voices of his children and grandchildren always made him smile and stir to respond.

Granddaughter Nicole came for the 86th birthday as well, and it was fun to have the eldest and the youngest grandkids together. Phil was sweet and attentive during the tea party the girls made for him, even though he was confined to bed. Joshua brought in a book of old cars after the tea party to chat with grand pop.

Joey prepared Phil to go outside in the wheelchair for his birthday meal- Phil loved being outside and ate pretty well. Afterwards when everyone went home it seemed that Phil was really ready for his last trip homeward. He did not eat nor drink anymore and yet, amazingly, he lived another 15 days. The whole family was alerted and they came night and day to say goodbye and thank their father for his life and devotion to them.

One night he told our son, Tim that he wanted him to prepare for the service at our church after his death. Phil knew he had only days to live and told Tim he wanted lots of hymns sung. Tim explained that he didn't know hymns like his parents did, so Phil told him to go out into the study and find some hymnbooks and practice with the family. Soon we heard the voices of our children and grandchildren singing hymns.

Saying goodbye is difficult but beautiful too. On the morning of October 12, 2012, just as the night watch nurse was leaving, I saw Phil's face and hands grow whiter. When I told the nurse, she called her office, telling them that she would be spending the day with me.

In just a few minutes, we saw Phil gently and quietly slip into the arms of Jesus. The nurse remarked about the tear that was slipping down his face. She said, "Oh Cindy, he is not finding it easy to leave you". I remember saying, "No Karen, the angel has come to take him to the Lord, he sees Jesus, his mother and father and his dear brother and he is thrilled to be safely home."

I thanked the Lord for Phil and for giving us the joy of seeing his final journey home with such peace and a sense of a 'job well done'!

When I think there are so many decisions to make or I don't know what to do, I remember one Sunday at church; Phil drew an illustration on his bulletin. He drew a pillar entwined by vines, and he said to me, with others watching,

"Remember Cindy, that the Lord through His Holy Spirit is the core of your life and He will never leave you nor forsake you. This pillar represents the Holy Spirit in our life and has been the center of our life together."

He pointed to the pillar.

He drew a vine, and then another encircling the pillar and off the top of the page. As he drew each leaf, he said, "This leaf represents key events in our lives. This leaf is when we met, this leaf is when we got married, this leaf is our first child, Becky, and these leaves are the other children and our ministry experiences. Notice that your vine stops here, and my vine grows off the top of the page. My vine is finished. Yours is still growing. You still have many more things to do."

He pointed to the leaves on my vine.

"You have a vital job in life, even after I am gone - so find it and finish it well."

Thank you Father, for helping me write these pages, and for giving me the strength to be obedient to whatever you call me to do. Thank you for Phil and our sixty years of life with you!

– Cindy Elizabeth Smith

The End

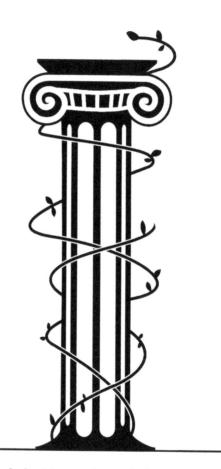

The Pillar and the Vines that Phil drew for Cindy.

These Papers Were In A Phil's File Labeled:
Keep To Share With Family

APPENDIX #1

The History of BEE: Its Beginnings By Dr. Jody Dillow

Dr. Jody Dillow addressed the staff of Biblical Education by Extension in January of 1996. This is a transcript of the tape made of that talk.

I was 35 years old when I went to Austria. I am 54 years old now. The Apostle Paul, when he launched his missionary journeys was probably in his late 40's, which in those days was probably considered a bit 'over the hill'.

So today, I am looking at a new future as we are all doing to some extent. We are all gathered here because of a common experience and a desire to capitalize on the experience which God gave us, working in these very unusual moments in history. This is what unites us.

In my own case, I came to Christ through the death of a girl with whom I was in love, and the testimony of her parents. Then it was Bud Hinkson, the director of Campus Crusade for Christ in the Northeast area, who discipled me and ultimately sent me to Dallas Seminary.

For many years, Bud, would come to Dallas and try to recruit me. I would ask him just what was it that he wanted me to do?

I recall him sitting in my living room, trying to make up a job description. That was not the job security I was looking for, if I were to move my family overseas. So I never took him seriously

Linda and I had prayed for many years about going to the mission field. I even applied to Inter Cristo, and asked 15 or 20 mission agencies for their brochures. But I never found anything that seemed to 'click'.

In the 1970's while I was in the doctoral program at Dallas Seminary, Bud Hinkson came through Dallas again. This time his latest scheme was to penetrate behind the Iron Curtain. He was gathering a team of people who would move to Vienna and he wanted to get some guys from Dallas to come and help him.

For me it was the 'same old, same old….trying to make up yet another job description in my living room'. I finally decided that I needed to go check it out. I said I would take a trip and was scheduled to go in January or February of 1977, just to visit.

About a week before the flight, I cancelled. I had never been overseas in my life and I just did not have peace about going. A few days later I received a phone call from Trinity Seminary: they invited me to teach Systematic Theology.

That was the field I had been studying, so I felt this was surely God's call upon my life. I was just finishing off my doctoral dissertation, when I got another phone call.

This call was from a medical doctor in Italy, Dr. Cesar, and he wanted to fly me to Vienna, Austria, at his expense to talk to him about how he could know Jesus Christ in a personal way!

I thought, perhaps Bud was right - God wants me to go to Vienna

- one way or another! Cesar had gotten my name from a contact in Dallas, and I was supposed to be the one who could help him with his intellectual questions.

Bud met me and we met with Dr. Cesar in the Hilton Hotel in Vienna for three days, but he went away sorrowful, unable to make the decision. Nonetheless, God used that experience to incline my heart toward Eastern Europe.

But, I had already made a commitment to teach at Trinity. So Linda and I packed up our family and went, but soon I began to feel ill at ease. It was a great experience, but still there was unrest.

I was feeling two things: First, if I was ever to go to the Mission field, this was the time before the kids got any older and second, I was beginning to see that the academic environment was not helpful in my own personal spiritual walk.

As I was working through these issues, Bud Hinkson showed up again and took me and Linda out to eat. He began talking about theological training by extensions, about launching a TEE program for pastors behind the Iron Curtain.

It was not a dramatic thing, but something just quietly 'clicked' inside of me. I turned to Linda and said, "Linda, we are going!" She about died but was willing because she had been praying about the mission field as well.

I informed Trinity that I would not be available for the following semester, and we raised support and were in Vienna within twelve weeks!

That first year, we did not even know what we were doing. I had the nebulous title of *Director of Training for Crusade*. We knew from the beginning it was sort of a 'non job', but it gave me an identity when I got there. The first year we studied German, and Linda did so much better than I that I felt like a failure. I floundered; my real heart beat was to get started training these pastors.

The following summer, Slavic Gospel Association and Navigators called a meeting in Vienna. About 30 missions were represented. The meeting's purpose was to explore the possibility of a united effort to launch an advanced program of Biblical Education in Eastern Europe.

I recall seeing Dr. Nic and some other people from Czechoslavia. It was a fantastic meeting. The Spirit of God was with us. We felt as though God had really met us and was about to do something spiritually significant in Eastern Europe.

I was just there as a 'Crusades representative' and I was wondering how all this was going to come together. We felt that we were a part of history. The Bible delivery missions had been delivering Bibles for years and now they needed to get some folks in there to teach from those Bibles.

Fred Holland led a discussion on how to do this teaching through extension. I was all ears learning about Eastern Europe and TEE.

During the meeting, Paul Stanley got up and said, "You know guys this is a very nice meeting; I have been to sessions like this many times, and I want to say that unless you have a leader, discussions like this will not go anywhere!"

I was sitting there wondering who I would be working for, because I really wanted to do this. Stanley then nominated me! I was sitting in the back of the room saying... "No, Stanley, I don't know anything about Eastern Europe, or TEE. I am here only as a learner!"

But, because I had a Ph.D after my name, I seemed qualified. The group reluctantly voted me in and Paul said to me, "Well Jody, it's all yours: you lead the rest of the seminar!"

I just about died: I had to stand up before these seasoned veterans of a dozen years or more in Eastern Europe and act like I knew what I was doing. At this point, I wanted to ring Paul Stanley's neck! I remember praying....'Help Lord, what am I to do?"

As I was walking forward, this big Russian, George Law, gave me a fist full of papers. It had organizational charts, goal statements, and job descriptions. Apparently, he had been stewing upon these things for a long time.

So I got up front and said..."Well, I think the goal of this organization should be..." And I bluffed my way through for most of the afternoon!

It was at this meeting that I met Al Bridges. Al was in Europe serving with the European Christian Mission, and was the only other person in the room who was available to work on this project full time!

The only reason we were chosen for leadership was because we were available at that time. The only reason I was the leader was because I had the Ph.D!

So Al and I began to work together. Al is a lot more reserved than I am. I am more the Aaron and he, the Moses. I am more public than he. I recall the first trip we made together to Romania, when I wondered if we would click. I liked this guy, but he didn't talk. He has loosened up tremendously since then!

Al is a true servant. From the beginning, he committed himself to making me successful. I would never have been able to serve in Vietnam or China, had it not been for Al.

For many years it was Jody and Al, working as one. Whatever decisions he made, I said, "Great". Whatever decisions I made, he said "Great". Over the years, Al has become my closest friend.

The first year of BEE, Crusade gave us an old office, and we hung out our shingle, calling ourselves the East European Center for Biblical Education by Extension. We worked out a four phase plan of implementation:

> Phase one: to develop goals and objectives and recruit five missions.
>
> Phase two: to develop curriculum (by 1991)
>
> Phase three: to launch a plan
>
> Phase four: to finish with everything indigenous by 1996

Our job at that early point was to make contacts and enlist the involvement of other missions. We wanted to recruit people, conceptualize the strategy, make contacts in Eastern Europe and raise support.

Well, God had a unique plan for us, and met our needs in dramatic ways. I will never forget the trip across Czechoslovakia with George Law. George spoke five languages and could go from Czech to German to Polish to Russian and French all in one sitting! He is a gifted genius, and took over the whole concept of translating curriculum into seven languages.

We learned of a program called Gutenberg, on the Apple computer, which we wanted to try. The translators could type the material into the Gutenberg directly, allowing us to cut translating time from five years to less than one.

The other thing we needed was a VAX computer. In those days it was a pretty big ticket item - about one hundred fifty thousand dollars. God provided an MIT Ph.D who decided to give us a year or two to set up the computer.

One hundred fifty thousand dollars was a huge amount to me at that time. I was having trouble raising my own personal support. The Lord brought along John Maisel, who jumped into the situation and began talking to some of our friends in Dallas. One man said that if we could get the other ninety thousand by December 31st, he would give us fifty.

We prayed and prayed. I shall never forget that phone call on December 30! John called me and said that God had provided the money, and a few weeks later we had that computer sitting in our office in Vienna.

The cost of running this operation began with nothing and went to five thousand a year and then to 1.5 million per year over four years.

Where was this money going to come from? In the providence of God, there were about 80 men in the North Dallas community that gave most of this money. These men were in Bible studies that Maisel and I taught in those years while I was in Dallas.

However, the big thing that pushed us over was when 'Nancy' first came to visit us in Vienna. She made a trip into Eastern Europe to check us out, asking the key pastors all over Romania what they knew about us. But no one talked!

Of course, in those days talking was a fearful thing to do. After we explained the situation, she made another trip and this time the pastors talked. They gave rave reviews of how the ministry was helping them, and her foundation gave us about fifty thousand dollars per month for a year, and then committed for the next year as well.

God used them to get us off the ground. God provided people, and money and one thing we learned: When we had a need, God provided the right person.

George Law and Ken Strespack were individuals God brought just at the right time. Bill Temple helped conceptualize the strategy and managed the country teams. Of course, John Maisel, who led our funding team and Hans Finzel, a fantastic administrator were others whom God brought us when we needed them. Whether we needed money or people or ideas, the Lord Jesus was there with all that was needed.

Personally, I have never had the opportunity to work with a group of people who were so gifted and unified, working together towards our common objectives. Those of you who were with us from those early days know how God was at work!

God had decided to do something in Eastern Europe: We just happened to be there at the right time. It was just the right idea, at the right time in history!

I will never forget when we first started the seminars. We were in Romania with twelve Baptist pastors, all under persecution from the authorities. I remember doing 'cleansing routes'; checking in windows to see if I was being followed. It was spooky in those early years of 1980.

We started a course called *Life of Christ*, which was a part of the New Testament survey. When we passed out the books, there was silence in the room, as the pastors held their books and stroked them. Then the leader said… "Never in the history of Romania, have we had such materials for the training of pastors!"

I saw them get brown paper to cover the books. They treated them as though they were precious jewels. At the end of the week Zaracko pulled me into his office and gave me an envelope, with the equivalent of a month's salary for him in Romania at the time. He said that we would have no idea how long they have prayed for these materials. He said that "it was like an angel from heaven to us. We want to give you something as a token of our appreciation!"

As we continued our strategy, God continued to bring people to help us in Vienna. When we left, there were about 200 people on staff and the intermission board, with directors of each of the missions ran that board. Al and I reported directly to that board.

It was October of 1987, and Al and I were running in the woods outside Vienna, both feeling rather antsy as most of our responsibilities were turned over to others. We were thinking; maybe God wants us to take this to other countries. When I asked Al what countries, he replied, "China!"

One morning as Linda and I were praying about China, we got a phone call from Nancy who wanted us to fly to London and meet with three key people there about launching BEE in China!

So Al and I brought a stack of papers about the history of the church in China, and spent a day talking about the situation in China. Three months later we went to China to see if there was indeed a place for us there.

The idea seemed right but not the timing. Two years later a businessman whom I had been meeting, asked me to lunch. He was from Hong Kong and had been praying about getting BEE curriculum translated into Chinese. He asked me to get him some numbers.

One week later I gave him my calculation: it would cost six hundred fifty thousand dollars. He said… "no problem!"

We went to Hong Kong to get things going. And Daniel Tran, who had been a student at Dallas Seminary, somehow heard that I was in Hong Kong, and came to see me.

Daniel had escaped Vietnam in 1972, as one of the boat people. For years he served as the voice for "Far Eastern" broadcast into Vietnam. He decided that he wanted to give the rest of his life to do BEE in Vietnam.

Tom Lewis, Al and I made a trip to Vietnam with him. Daniel would call the top guys in six different denominations and they came to meet with us almost immediately. It was like going with the Pied Piper, we immediately had his credibility. Through the providence of God we were able to get BEE going in Vietnam almost instantly.

The one point I want to leave with you is that I am in awe with what God has done! The glory and the honor is His. I think that if we are willing to take a step in faith and trust Him, He will do great things through us!

I have often been filled with doubt, but when I trust Him and step out, He provides the people, the creativity, the strategy, and the money. Whatever is needed He is there!

What's Going On In Romania?

Based on Phil's notes and files, this is a summary of the political and spiritual realities in Romania prior to the collapse of the Soviet Union.

The Mad Massacre in Romania

A tall fence encloses three square miles of real estate in the heart of Bucharest the Romanian capitol. A few months ago, this was the city's noted Uranus quarter, the pride of Romanians, featuring select buildings of their nation's supreme architectural heritage. Then came the mammoth bulldozers and cranes - demolition teams that devoured grand museums, stunning monasteries, ancient churches and majestic old buildings.

This mindless cultural massacre was ordered by the country's president, Nicolae Ceausescu, to make way for a concrete colossus to glorify the "twenty years of enlightenment' under his autocratic communist yoke. Over the ruins of the Uranus quarter will rise a civic center, a Victory of Socialism Boulevard, and a public square to accommodate half a million people for his outlandish Nazi-style rallies. In the wake of his arrogant move, art was destroyed, jobs were eliminated and more than 40,000 people were forced from their homes, many with only 24 hours' notice.

Even by communist standards the project is obscene. Yet it is just one of the staggering examples of the personality cult this land's dictator has created. Seeking power, wealth and adulation, the 67-year-old Ceausescu demands his country to focus on him. He spares no self-indulgence because he believes he is the 'great predestined one; a 'paragon of reason and clear-sightedness; the "homeland's hero of heroes."

The state owned press devotes half its newsprint to Ceausescu idolatry, likening him to Alexander the Great, Caesar and Napoleon. From a Biblical viewpoint, his megalomania reminds one of Nebuchadnezzar. His portrait adorns the wall of the office and public places everywhere. His ubiquitous visage smiles down from billboards even on rural roads. "The Ceausescu Era," declared a recent resolution of the Romanian Communist Party, "Is the most brilliant in the nation's history."

In reality, Ceausescu's Romania is a society governed by fear, where the Marxist state dictates nearly every waking moment of the hapless citizen's existence. Economically, Ceausescu has reduced this nation of 22.6 million to poverty despite its abundance of natural resources.

Ceausescu's Rise to Power: There were a paltry amount of Communist Party members in 1944, when the Russian army rolled into Romania. One was Nicolae Ceausescu, a shoemaker. The third of ten children in a poor peasant family, he joined the then-outlawed party in his mid-teens and became one of its youth leaders. His activities landed him in prison, where he came under the wing of fellow prisoner Gheorghe Gheorghiu-Dej, the man who would lead the communist Romanian Workers' Party from 1948 until 1965.

Under his mentor, the youthful zealot had a meteoric rise. And when the old dictator died in 1965, Ceausescu had little difficulty maneuvering into the seat of power and fostered a personality cult and violently suppressed any shred of opposition.

A Timeline of Terror

1965 – Ceausescu became leader of the Communist Party

1968 – He denounced the Soviet invasion of Czechoslovakia

1975 – USA grants Romania most-favored nation status

1985-1986 – Severe austerity programs lead to food shortages and widespread vpower outages

1987 – Romanian Army crushes labor demonstrations and occupies power plants in Brasov.

1989 – December – Demonstrations in Timisoara in support of dissident pastor, Aszlo Tokes triggers bloody national uprising. Nicolae and Elena Ceausescu try to flee with some of their wealth, but are caught, tried and executed by a firing squad on Christmas day for crimes against the state.

More astonishing, in this land known historically as the Balkan breadbasket, is the chronic shortage of food because so much— over $1 billion worth a year-is exported to pay Ceausescu's bills.

When news of his citizens' dissatisfaction reached Ceausescu, his response was one of perfect disdain: it would do Romanians good because they were overweight!

Indeed, when it comes to internal dissent, Ceausescu' response is brutal. His ruthless Securitate, employing over 500,000 agents and informers, rivals the Soviet Union's KGB in efficiency. Thousands of political, religious or other activists have been put into prisons, work camps and psychiatric hospitals, or have simply disappeared.

Most Orwellian of all, however, has been Ceausescu's 'baby boom' diktat. In 1972, he set the country a goal: by the year 2000 it must have a population of 30 million. To this end he banned contraception and made abortion illegal. The birthrate quickly increased threefold. But with perpetual economic austerity, women were unwilling to have big families, and illegal abortion became a principal means of birth control. Despite jail threats of mother and doctor, if caught, by 1983 abortions were more numerous than live births.

Clearly, he is a ruthless and power hungry despot.

Toilet Paper from Bibles

One of the greatest grievances of the Hungarian Reformed Church in Romania is that it cannot obtain Bibles and hymnals. These two most important tools of religious life have been simply out of print for decades.

The customary question of the border guards and custom officers when you enter Romania is… "Do you have guns, drugs or Bibles?" After the Second World War, according to the Helsinki

Accords, Romania is under obligation to permit the reprint of Bible and hymnals. They have made it clear also that if such reprints would be impossible due to lack of modern printing technology or lack of paper, they (churches in West) would be prepared to supply their Protestant brethren with Bibles and Hymnals.

Under Western pressure, the Ceausescu regime gave permission to the World Reformed Alliance to send 20,000 Bibles to the Hungarian Reformed church in Romania. The leadership of the Alliance considered it a triumph of patient and persistent church diplomacy.

However, the fate of the 20,000 Bibles was shrouded in mystery. The leadership of the Hungarian Reformed Church of Romania could never give a proper account of their distribution.

After a long silence, the Bibles reappeared in Romania in the form of toilet paper. The mystery of the Hungarian Bible was finally revealed. It was observed in the regions with large Hungarian populations that the toilet paper, which was extremely scarce on the market, revealed words in Hungarian such as Esau, Jeremiah and God.

The 20,000 Hungarian Bibles were obviously sent to the paper-mill in Braila to be recycled for the manufacture of toilet tissue paper.

But as often happens in Communist Romania, the pulp mill did a rather shoddy job. The excellent quality of western bibliophile paper and print could not be recycled by the crude pulp mill. Shreds of paper, with original words and letters remained almost intact on the final toilet paper products.

The action of the Ceauseseu Regime clearly reflects its contempt of religious life in general, and of the Hungarian Reformed minority in particular. There were many book burnings in history. However, such a deliberately barbarian and cynical deed which would use the Holy Scripture for the making of toilet paper is unique in human history.

Romania: The Persecuted Church: At the Heart of the Revolution

For months Laszlo Tokes, pastor of the Hungarian Reformed Church in Timisoara, Romania, had been harassed by the Securitate (secret police) because of his outspoken criticism of the brutal regime of Nicolae Ceausescu. But on December 16, when Securitate officers arrived at the church, his supporters formed a human blockade to prevent his arrest and deportation. What began as a congregation's protest in support of its pastor became the nine-day revolution that cost thousands of lives but brought liberate—freedom—to the Romanian people.

That the beginning of the revolution was sparked by the dissent of a pastor and his congregations is not surprising. During the years of the oppressive communist regime, the witness and perseverance of the evangelical church was one of the few voices of dissent in Romania. In spite of severe repression, the evangelical presence in Romania was one of the fastest growing in all of Europe, with roughly a half-million members in Baptist, Brethren, and Pentecostal denominations, as well as an evangelical group within the

Romanian Orthodox Church.

Dissent found its home in the clandestine activities of believers; underground printing, Bible distribution, and small-group Bible studies. Despite attempts by the Securitate to curtail such activities through terror and intimidation, many church leaders and members continued in their endeavors. As one respected Pentecostal leader from Bucharest said, "Christianity in our country is like a nail: the harder you strike it, the deeper it goes!"

By its very nature, the church's message posed a threat to the Ceausescu regime, because it recognized a higher authority than the state. And many outside observers and believers in the country say it freed Romanians - who faced gun barrels in their protests for freedom - from the fear of death.

Although the revolution seemed spontaneous, a number of evangelicals within the country had felt for some time that change was not far off. According to one leader near Cluj, a secret meeting was held in that city in November in which seven intellectuals from various evangelical denominations met and discussed the formation of a Christian league to concentrate efforts against the government.

A number of leaders have also testified to the importance prayer played in bringing freedom to Romania. According to another Baptist lay pastor from the city of Cluj, Tuesday evening prayer meetings began in 1980 among the Baptists throughout the country. The meetings' focus was found in Acts 3:19....."that the Lord would bring a time of refreshing to Romania"!

"God has turned his face to us!" were the cries heard in Timisoara on December 20, when the Securitate withdrew from shooting at the crowds gathered in the city square. Numerous church leaders led the crowds there in mass recitals of the Lord's Prayer during the next several days. On December 22, Peter Dugalescu, a Baptist pastor from Timisoara, stood to address the crowd in the square. Before he started preaching, news of Ceausescu's flight was announced. Dugalescu then led the crowd of over 100,000 in prayer.

Other spontaneous and massive prayer responses occurred in the cities of Oradea and Constanta. In Cluj, a group of Christian youth went to the train station to sing Christmas carols on Christmas Eve. When they arrived at the train station another spontaneous prayer meeting took place. With the sound of shooting in the city square in the background, everyone at the station knelt in prayer for the country.

APPENDIX #3

Letters of Encouragement

To Phil and Cindy

November 1992

We send you greetings from Moscow! Time flies so fast; it is already more than half a year that we spent without you. We miss you!

I am now looking at a photo which brings back many recollections of the time we spent together in Moscow. Remember our first Christian Christmas celebration as a church? I can still see Cindy singing that song,"Quiet night, Holy Night". How blessed we were with your ministry with us. And what joy to see the abundance of the fruit from that time, like Natasha who came to Christ through Cindy. She is a sweet Christian and a great encouragement for us all now.

And thank you Phil, for the personal input to my heart and life. You taught me so many things. We have a great loving church here because of you two, and our loving God.

There are many on staff at our church now; we even have two pastors, and a pastor to women. We are working on the follow up of new believers and many other couples and families help in the work. Thank you for all your labors and love shown to us.

We have seen so many changes since you were here. We had

to move to another hall, which is smaller, but still very nice. There is a great spirit of love and worship and we now have a time of fellowship after our service. Because we meet in a hall at the Moscow Linguistic University, we have a really great outreach, with services nearly every day. We are now beginning a cell group project to meet throughout the city.

The Lord has been very gracious to me. Since I am now studying at the St. James Bible College in Moscow, I am happily studying the Bible every day, and am learning to take notes like you taught me!

My dear Mom is doing great and is very busy with the church. She sends her love to you and is praying for you to be able to go to China. Her sister Flora is using Cindy's material for teaching. Flora's pastor liked the study material so much that he is using it is his own church!

I do hope to hear from you some time. I trust you are doing great. I love you - you are very special to me. Thank you!

Your brother in Christ, Nick K

Another letter was from Eleanor who was a translator in Minsk, Belarus-Russia, and was hired by our students who knew her as a Professor of English at the Technical University. She knew very little about the Bible but she was eager to assist us.

The pastors were studying our course on Galatians and Romans, covering the first few chapters of Romans in our discussion. During a tea break, Eleanor turned and asked me to explain how a person could be saved. For the next half hour I answered her questions and shared the basic truths of the gospel. When I asked if she wanted to receive Christ she said that she needed time to think.

After returning to the States, I corresponded with her and kept her on my prayer list for years. A colleague took an English Bible to her and she sent us a gracious letter of appreciation, telling us that she was reading the Bible.

Recently, when I wrote to her, I was excited to receive her reply. Here are her words:

> "I am absolutely thrilled to get your letter after all these years. It's so nice of you to remember me! I work at the Belarusian State University at the Department of International Relations, teaching future diplomats. Dear Phil, I remember you telling me, "God loves you! At that time it was difficult for me to understand. Thank God, you impressed me very much, and you made me think, and I have come to Him. Last May I was baptized. Dear Phil, I am so grateful to him that he gave me the opportunity to meet you and Cindy, to listen to you, and open my ears to hear you. God bless you.'

> Eleanor D

From Vietnam we received another letter:

> Dear Pastor Phil,

> Thank you for the studies you left with me. Reading them over and over and digging into the Word is bringing me to my knees before the Lord. Studying what God requires of His men is powerful.

> Thank you for sharing with me and for showing me practical ways to live before Christ and my people. I pray for you as you continue to write. May God continue to bless and use you. I consider you as my Father.

This pastor came to visit me after Phil died and I let him choose more of Phil's books and writings to take home with him. I have done this with all those who come to visit. Some guests also select a toy car from Phil's collection!

Another Vietnamese pastor who visited recently, requested that I keep all the files on Vietnam for him to use in writing his graduate study thesis one day.

He reminded me that through the years he had not been able to keep such papers as the government made frequent visits to destroy studies and papers. It was a delight when he pointed to pictures of the women in our classes and told me where they were serving today!

"In the fear of the Lord there is strong confidence, and His children will have a place of refuge. The fear of the Lord is a fountain of life, to turn one away from the snares of death." Proverbs 14:26-27

LEGACY (UNDESERVING)

Words and Music by Chuck Butler, written for Phil Smiths' 80th
birthday 2006.

Years go by, they fly just like the wind
Joy and tears, are both teachers in the end

When the storm has come, and it will
When all is said and done, you might listen still

He's given me a legacy
To pass on down
It'll make the blind to see
An' turn this world around

He offers an inheritance
That we don't deserve
Some would even question Him
But that's the way He works

CHORUS....

Undeserving...drink from the fountain
Come unworthy...to the banquet
Bring your burdens...He will lift them
Disappointments....melt away.